A Matter of
Life and Death

The Secrets of
Shrewsbury Cemetery

A Matter of Life and Death

The Secrets of
Shrewsbury Cemetery

by
Peter Francis

Logaston Press

LOGASTON PRESS
Little Logaston Woonton Almeley
Herefordshire HR3 6QH
logastonpress.co.uk

First published by Logaston Press 2006
Copyright © Peter Francis 2006

ISBN 1 904396 58 5
(978 1 904396 58 1)

Set in Times New Roman by Logaston Press
and printed in Great Britain by
Oaklands Book Services, Gloucestershire

Front cover illustration: Shrewsbury Cemetery

*This book is dedicated to the memory of my parents,
John and Sheila*

Contents

Individuals mentioned in the text whose names are given in bold lettering are buried or commemorated in Shrewsbury Cemetery. The number in brackets after their names relate to the Cemetery plan on page *xi*.

Acknowledgements

Writing this book has been very much a labour of love for me. Researching it has taken me down many historical roads and by-ways. Some have ultimately proved to be cul-de-sacs, whilst others have opened up whole new arenas of knowledge and interest. I have been helped by many different people along the way. There is one person, however, without whom this book would never have been written. It was my friend Michael Webb who first shared with me some of the secrets waiting to be revealed amongst the gravestones and memorials of Shrewsbury Cemetery. The help and information he has provided with a number of sections of this book has been incalculable.

Below is a list of those to whom I also owe special thanks with details of the areas in which they gave particular help:

Jonathan Morgans of Wellspring Apostolic church (Belle Vue cemetery); staff of Fleet Library (Ft Lt Robert Jenkins); Robert Pringle (Burnell House); Michael Hulme of Shropshire Family History Society (Policemen Farlow, Howell and Lear); staff of Lincoln Cathedral Library (Edward King); Peter Lobbenberg (Hans Lobbenberg and Corsets Silhouette Ltd); David Etherington (Hans Lobbenberg's chess career); Toby Neal of the *Shropshire Star* (John Morris' death); Mark Dickson of Shrewsbury School (Shrewsbury School footballers); Mr John Bowdler (J.C.H. Bowdler); Hugh Kent of Kingsland Grange School (War Graves); Chris Rogers, Alfie Coglianese and Michael Dennis (translations of gravestone epitaphs); Tom Wall and Russell Nimmo for proof-reading and valuable editorial comment; and my wife Julia for help, support and advice throughout the whole project.

All the illustrations are the author's with the following exceptions for which thanks are given for the permission to use them in this publication: Jonathan Morgans for that on p.6, Shrewsbury Museums Service for the portraits on pp.15 and 16 (bottom); David Trumper for those on pp.17, 20 (bottom), 24, 26, 88 and 110; Shropshire Archives for those on pp.33, 38, 39, 40, 43 and 112; Gordon Dickins for that on p.51; Geoff Harrison for that on p.52; The *Shropshire Star* for those on pp.56, 57, 79, 80 and 103; Lincoln Cathedral for that on p.69; Angela Marshall for that on p.78; Shrewsbury School for the top photograph on p.95; Gareth M. Davies for the bottom photograph on p.95 and Katy Shoesmith for the map on p.100.

Introduction

It might make one in love with death, to think
that one should be buried in so sweet a place.
from *Adonais* by Percy Bysshe Shelley

Places of burial hold a certain undeniable fascination. Archaeologists who
excavate prehistoric burial mounds invariably uncover much which can talk
to us about the customs, beliefs and lives of our ancestors and their attitudes
to death and burial. Such attitudes vary much in different parts of the world
and have done so even more throughout history. In Victorian England death
was surrounded by much pomp, ceremony and artistic endeavour and it
was amongst such attitudes that Shrewsbury and other latter day urban
cemeteries arose. Since then, people's perceptions have changed further and,
in particular, the mindless slaughter of two World Wars has impacted greatly
on our views of the commemoration of those who have 'passed on'. All of
this, and much more, can be traced by the simple (and enjoyable) expedient of
wandering around any of the many cemeteries which lie in our cities, towns
and villages.

To think of cemeteries as simply places of the dead, however, is to
undervalue them and deny the continuity of memory which they so vividly
represent. Like an individual person, a human community is woven out
of its memory and when we bury the dead, we invariably remember their
achievements, their sense of humour, peculiarities and failings, the ways in
which they laid out their lives and faced fortune and tragedy. By such means
we perpetuate the memory of our ancestors — perhaps the strongest cord of
human continuity, lying at the very heart of our deepest values.

Each gravestone and memorial in a cemetery has a story to tell, to those
who seek it. Collectively, such stories weave the fabric of our communal
history. In Shrewsbury Cemetery lie writers, performers, civic, church and
business leaders, campaigners, military heroes and illustrious sportsmen.
Some who are buried there took their own lives or gave theirs to save others.
Some memorials are to those who died in disastrous fires, rail crashes and
flying accidents, and some died far from home in the service of their country.
Well known and familiar names can be found there, as well as those whose
stories and achievements have been lost over time. All, however, have played
their part and earned their place in the history of our community.

Peter Francis

*One of a number of poignant memorials to babies
who died at Shrewsbury Hospital*

All of the Cemetery is still open to the public and opening times are displayed at the main entrance. Care however must be taken if you leave the pathways. The tightly packed gravestones of the older sections of the Cemetery, in particular, mean that it is important to take your time and watch your step. Some graves have also been fenced off for very good health and safety reasons and such barriers must always be respected.

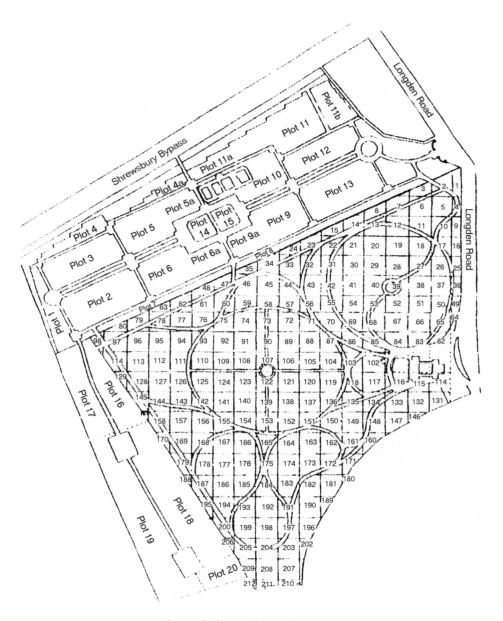

Plan of Shrewsbury Cemetery

The grave of Amy Vincent, 'Lady Principal of the Vernacular and English Girls School, Batticaloa, Ceylon'

1   ORIGINS OF SHREWSBURY CEMETERY

The 19th century saw huge and dramatic demographic changes in the UK which brought with them a host of related problems. The population rose from 16 million to in excess of 40 million during the century and the proportion of people living in towns and cities increased from less than 20% to over 75%. Questions such as where people would live and work, who would produce enough food for their tables and, indeed, where would their dead be buried where forced to the forefront of public debate.

As early as the 1660s, John Evelyn had argued that churchyards in the City of London were already over-full and 'an affront to public decency'. In his Diary he described churchyards as being 'filled up with the congestion of dead bodies one above the other, to the very top of the walls ... so that the churches seem to be built in pits.' When plans were laid for re-building London after the Great Fire, they included 'cemeteries seated in the outskirts of the town' and the banning of further burials in churchyards. It was to be the 19th century, however, before such ideas finally came to fruition.

The model for the Victorian cemetery movement in England was to come from Paris. By 1784, the great burial ground of central Paris — the Cimetiere des Innocents — had been in use since the Middle Ages, and in that year it was finally closed due, according to one source, to the danger of disease and the smell from the putrefying bodies. Soon after, almost all the ancient burial grounds in the city followed suit. In 1786 and '87 the accumulated bones of centuries, said to represent around two million bodies, were taken to underground limestone quarries which became known as The Catacombs. Three new cemeteries in the north, south and east of Paris were opened. Père Lachaise (named after the original owner of the land) was the first to open and was the largest and most important of the three. Its hilly grounds were surrounded by high walls and formal avenues, and serpentine walks were laid out in a picturesque terrain. The first burial there took place in 1804.

The campaign to establish such cemeteries in England did not really get underway until the 1820s. In Liverpool, Low Hill cemetery was open by 1825, though it was soon largely replaced by the Cemetery of St James only a mile away. In different ways, both the Liverpool cemeteries made use of a unique architectural style for their buildings and expressed 'affective qualities that originated in sentiment and Romantic attitudes towards the dead'. As such, they mirrored the style of Père Lachaise across the Channel. New English cemeteries in Norwich, Manchester and Liverpool were all established by means of private enterprise. Joint Stock companies were set up, money raised by the issue of shares and dividends paid out. It was not until 1830, however, that the first public meeting took place in London to discuss the possibility of similar developments there. It was organised by the campaigner George Frederick Carden and led, in 1832, to the establishment of the General Cemetery Company. The 54 acre Kensal Green Cemetery was finished in 1837 and by 1840 shares in the General Cemetery Company had more than doubled their original value of £25.

The basic theme of the design of these early cemeteries was of a garden or rural park. Others soon appeared in the cities of Newcastle (1831) and Leeds (1835) and in the years between 1837 and 1840 Norwood, Highgate and Nunhead cemeteries followed Kensal Green in serving the city of London. Provincial towns such as Cheltenham (1830) were not excluded and in 1840 an Act of Parliament authorised the establishment of the first cemetery in Shrewsbury.

Non-conformists led the way in cemetery building in England. Companies were established and offered to sell burial plots to all-comers. Such policies resulted largely from the need to satisfy share-holders. Church law, however, said that any burial ground used by Anglicans had to be consecrated by the diocesan Bishop of the parish from which the dead came. This led to friction, and at Abney Park, Stoke Newington, congregations went ahead without the requisite Act of Parliament in an attempt to lower burial costs for the working classes. Despite this, cemeteries continued to largely serve the privileged few, and failed, therefore, to provide any real solution to the problem of burying the urban dead. Clearly this could not continue.

George Arthur Walker was a doctor with a surgery which served a densely populated part of London — a maze of courts and alleys hidden away near Drury Lane, The Strand and Covent Garden. He was familiar with the difficulties of urban burial from his home town of Nottingham and had visited Père Lachaise. Some of the worst of London's burial grounds were situated in the area in which he worked. They were hemmed in by buildings and tight up against houses and tenements. Many were tiny, only a few hundred square yards, and even the largest were pitifully small for the populations they served.

In 1841, Dr Walker published *Gatherings from Graveyards*, a book which placed the crisis of urban burial before its middle class readers in stark, unrelenting terms. In the corner of the St Giles burial ground, he said,

2

is the 'bone house' which is a large round pit; into this had been shot, from a wheelbarrow, the but-partly decayed inmates of smashed coffins. Here, in this place of 'Christian burial', you may see human heads, covered with hair; and here, in this 'consecrated ground' are human bodies with flesh still adhering to them. On the north side a man was digging a grave; he was quite drunk, so indeed were all the grave diggers we saw ... a child's coffin, which had stopped the man's progress, had been cut, longitudinally, right in half; and there lay the child ... wrapped in its shroud, resting upon the part of the coffin which remained. The shroud was but little decayed ...

In burial ground after burial ground, Walker saw graves violated, bodies dismembered and exposed, simple human dignity ignored and outraged. But these were as nothing compared to what he found in the burial place under Enon Chapel, Clement's Lane, established as a private venture in 1823. In a space 59 feet long and 29 feet wide and some 6 feet in depth, separated from the chapel above by nothing more substantial than floorboards, 'Graveyard Walker' as he became known estimated that 12,000 bodies had been placed. The crisis Walker described, as he was well aware, was only one part of an urban emergency which encompassed open sewers, reeking water supplies, undrained tenements and overflowing cess-pits. Walker concluded that the only solution must involve strong legislative action to close urban burial grounds and provide cemeteries outside cities and available to all.

In 1842 the Poor Law Commissioners produced their Report on the Sanitary Conditions of the Labouring Classes of Great Britain. In it they argued that the existing situation was both morally and medically indefensible and that urgent remedies were needed. These, the Commissioners believed, could only be provided centrally by the State, not by private companies. The Report proposed that:

- urban burial grounds be closed;
- burial within church buildings be forbidden by law;
- cemeteries be established outside towns, near to canals and railways, and laid out with formal landscaping;
- bodies be kept in sanitary conditions whilst awaiting burial; and
- communities, congregations and trades be allowed to apply for their own exclusive areas.

The Report received much attention but in reality very little happened. The increase in cemetery building in the second half of the 1840s still resulted very largely from private enterprise.

In August 1848, the first Public Health Act received royal assent. It laid the foundations for all public health measures up to and after the First World

War and began a process which led to the establishment of public cemeteries throughout Britain. Local Boards of Health were established with powers to close burial grounds if they were a danger to health, approve new cemeteries and establish receiving houses for the dead. In practice they had little real effect. Nevertheless, the argument for the establishment of public cemeteries, funded by public money, was won.

There followed, in July 1852, the influential Metropolitan Burial Act which empowered the Privy Council to close any place of burial in London (without the need to show it was a danger to health) and ensured that no new burial ground in or near the city could be opened without the permission of the Secretary of State. Parishes (or groups of parishes) could set up Burial Boards to build new cemeteries funded out of the Poor Rate and manage them once they had been opened. In August 1853 powers contained in the Act were extended to the rest of England and Wales.

This legislation had at last provided an effective answer to the burial crisis of the 1830s and '40s. It ensured a system of public burial which essentially has survived to the present day and, crucially, with the necessary powers fixed firmly at a local level. The great majority of Victorian cemeteries were established by these Burial Boards and the building of private cemeteries virtually ceased. In the wake of the Act, Burial Boards sprung up with remarkable speed in new cities, market towns, seaside resorts and even village parishes. To a large extent, the movement in Shrewsbury which eventually led to the opening of the General Cemetery mirrored these national developments.

Early steps centred round the Abbey Garden — a patch of ground at the east end of the Abbey church (not to be confused with the Abbey Gardens next to the Wakeman School). Plans had been announced to sell off the area in small individual plots. This prompted a group of local gentlemen to purchase the whole of the Garden with a view to it becoming the town's first public cemetery. Their main aim in this seems to have been to ensure that the Abbey did not, as a result of the sale, become surrounded and hemmed in by a host of small buildings. It was inevitable however that such a development would go at least some way towards easing Shrewsbury's own 'burial crisis'. As this was happening prior to the passing of the 1852 Metropolitan Burial Act, subsequently extended nationwide, it was a private enterprise affair.

The Abbey Cemetery Company was founded and money raised by the sale of £50 shares; the necessary Act of Parliament was obtained in 1840 and the plans began to fall into place. The establishment of the Abbey Cemetery was warmly welcomed in the local press, where concern about the over-crowded state of the town's churchyards was expressed in vivid language, typical of the time. The new cemetery would, it was said, prevent 'the sacrilegious disturbance of a mass of putrefying substance in some instance aroused before

4

the operation of nature could assimilate them to their kindred earth, in the limited space allotted for that purpose within a town closely encompassed by dwellings.' The cemetery was consecrated on 18 October 1841 by the Bishop of Lichfield and, soon afterwards, workmen were busy planting shrubs and evergreens and laying out walks. The first burial was that of Robert Stanway, a one year old infant who was laid to rest just below the Abbey's east window.

The venture, however, was far from being a great success. Only 148 burials took place in the years between 1841 and 1888 when it was sold back to the Abbey and used as an extension to the graveyard. The final burials to take place were of three members of the Watkis family from Abbeydale, Abbey Foregate buried within the space of one week. Their grave can still be seen in the far north east corner of the old cemetery.

The next significant development in Shrewsbury took place in nearby Belle Vue, where, in 1852, the growing non-conformist community in the town opened their own cemetery. It was situated on the Belle Vue Road, opposite the junction with South Hermitage. A small stone mortuary chapel in the Early English style was constructed in the centre of the two acre plot. The cemetery was managed by Richard Maddox of Besford House in Trinity Street; he had been a leading light in the movement to establish the cemetery and was a member of the family which owned and ran the well-known Maddox's store in Shrewsbury town centre. The chapel was partly burnt down by children in

Graves in the Abbey Garden cemetery
with the Watkis family memorial in the foreground

The opening of the Belle Vue Apostolic chapel in 1949 with the mortuary chapel still to be seen in the background

1943, and in 1949 the present Apostolic chapel was moved there brick by brick from its original site in Minsterley. Some of the graves from its time as a non-conformist cemetery can still be seen at various points around the site, as can the foundations of the old chapel.

Not long after the opening of the Belle Vue cemetery, in response to the Metropolitan Burial Act and in line with many other towns throughout the country, Shrewsbury established its own Burial Board. The Board comprised some 54 members, nine from each parish in the town — St Mary's, St Chad's, Holy Cross, St Julian's, St Alkmund's and Meole Brace. It seems to have been, almost inevitably, a rather cumbersome and bureaucratic body. Nevertheless, by 1856 it had achieved its purpose of building a new general cemetery to serve the people of Shrewsbury. At times progress toward that end was slow and difficult and friction between different factions, denominations and churches became almost commonplace. Serious accusations of impropriety were made against individuals, and battles fought in the pages of the local press.

Much heated debate centred around the choice of contractor to 'layout and plant' the land, for which three tenders were submitted. Although the most expensive, the tender of Messrs Groves of Shrewsbury was initially accepted by the Board. They seem to have been swayed by the arguments of a Mr Edward Hughes, that being local townsmen they would be more likely to earn the confidence of the Board. The approval of the Secretary of State, Sir George Grey, was still needed however and, perhaps not surprisingly, Sir George rejected the Board's proposal to accept the highest rather than the lowest tender. The initial decision was over-turned but not before Mr Hughes' well-known links with Messrs Groves had been vigorously pointed out by his opponents. Following a meeting of the Board on 4 October 1855, the *Shrewsbury Chronicle* published a partisan piece entitled Defeat of the Clique. In it they wondered, 'how Mr Hughes can again have the effrontery to argue the way he did.' They expressed equal surprise that he had managed to find twelve men to vote with him. His opinions were 'not at all consonant with independence and reason' said the *Chronicle*.

On 1 April 1856 a 'melancholy accident' occurred at the Cemetery site. A sub-contractor, Joseph Harris, left his two brothers, Thomas and Samuel, and another workman to continue the sinking of a well near to the Cemetery chapel buildings. Thomas was working some 25 feet below the surface, but with only the first 18 inches lined with bricks. Without warning, the soil from behind the brickwork gave way and instantly engulfed him. His brother Samuel made valiant attempts to rescue him, injuring himself in the process, but to no avail. Thomas's body was not finally extracted until 8pm the following day.

At their meeting on 11 April, contributions were invited from Burial Board members to a collection for the dead man's family He was said to have left two orphaned children one of whom was an 'idiot'. At the same time, however, the Board sought desperately to distance themselves from any responsibility. At the inquest, held at the Red Barn public house opposite the Cemetery entrance, the jury declined to apportion any blame and recorded a simple verdict of 'accidental death'.

An undercurrent of tension between members of the established church and the non-conformist community in Shrewsbury also runs throughout the Board's discussions. One aspect of this related to which section of the Cemetery grounds should be set aside for non-conformist burials. The proposal was that this should be an area to the west of the chapel building at the higher end of the Cemetery. A Mr Bloxham 'most decidedly objected' to giving up the best part of the Cemetery to the 'dissenters'. He was supported by the Revd J.J. Rogerson who sought to point out that the non-conformist population of Shrewsbury represented 'one fourth or less' of the community.

These comments led to a letter from 'A Dissenter' published in the *Shrewsbury Chronicle* of 11 April 1856. The anonymous writer asked: 'When will the English open their eyes and throw off priestcraft?' Referring to the existence of the Dissenter Cemetery in Belle Vue, he went on, 'Dissenters feel it rather hard not only to be compelled to pay for another cemetery but to be taunted with the falsehood that they do not amount to one fourth of the population and to find the most eligible spot not allotted to them.' He ended, however, on a more philosophical note: 'E'er long all distinctions will cease whether our bodies be buried in rather expensive ground duly consecrated by a Bishop and properly separated by a wall or unostentatiously laid at Belle Vue cemetery.'

This tension between church and chapel also surfaced at a higher level, with the Bishop of Hereford, who was to consecrate the cemetery, indicating that he wished the roofline of the Dissenters chapel to be lower than that of the consecrated Anglican one. He did however withdraw his objections when it was pointed out that this would result in an overall deterioration in the appearance of the buildings. The group of buildings at the north end of the

The Cemetery chapel

Cemetery stand today much as they did when originally constructed. They consist of two 'lodges' designed to house cemetery staff, a covered entrance area and a chapel, and between them a pleasant square grassed area surrounded by cloister-like corridors. The non-conformist chapel seems to have stood in this grassy area but has long since been demolished.

The man chosen to design and oversee the construction of the Cemetery buildings was local architect **Samuel Pountney Smith (190)**. He acquired this responsibility in somewhat dramatic circumstances. The Burial Board had announced a competition with an award to be granted for the best design. Sensibly, however, they reserved the right to either adopt the winning design or not. A large number of entries was received and one even selected for the award, when Pountney Smith entered the room and announced: 'Gentlemen, I know I am too late to compete for the premium but here is my plan which is at your service if you think proper.' It is said that the superiority of his design was so apparent at first glance that it was adopted there and then. The design envisaged that the chapels be built in grey stone in the fashionable Gothic style. When built, it was described in a contemporary guide book as noted for its 'quality of detail, originality of plan and excellence of design.'

Smith had not been born to the profession. His father was an innkeeper at Munslow in the Corvedale, and he learnt the trades of a builder and architect working with his uncle, John Smallman, at Quatford. In 1840 he set up his own business in Coleham and soon built up an extensive practice; he also became a prominent figure in the life of the town, serving as its mayor in 1873/74. As an architect, his great speciality was 'revival' styles at a time when the Victorian craze for Gothic led to a wave of church building and restoration. He was a sympathetic restorer and much of his building work which has survived looks deceptively original. He died, after three months paralysis, on 5 November 1883, aged 71. Today Pountney Gardens off Belle Vue Road, recalls his links with the area.

General regulations for the efficient running of the Cemetery were also needed. The Secretary, Mr Peele, was instructed to examine those in use elsewhere. He reported that the best example he had come across were in use in Bradford. It was these which formed the basis for the regulations adopted in Shrewsbury. They covered a wide range of eventualities, including that:

- no burials to be made before 10am and none on a Sunday, unless approved by the officiating minister;
- where more than one body was placed in a grave, 18 inches of earth must be between them;
- only wooden coffins allowed;
- no burials were to take place within 10 feet of the chapel or fences or lodge buildings;
- in the event of an offensive smell issuing from any corpse, that the officiating minister could order that it not be brought into the chapel;
- no children under ten would be admitted to the Cemetery unless in the care of a responsible person and no dogs would be admitted at all.

General view of the Cemetery buildings

In addition, the Burial Board reserved the right to levy a fine of £5 on 'anyone who damages any part of the cemetery or puts any bill up, defaces or damages any monument, plays at any game or sport, discharges arms except at a military funeral, disturbs any person assembled there or commits any nuisance.'

On Tuesday 26 November 1856 the Cemetery was duly consecrated. The ceremony was carried out by the Bishop of Hereford, as it was situated in Meole Brace parish and therefore within the Diocese of Hereford. This was despite the fact that the major part of the town fell within the Diocese of Lichfield (and today does so entirely). The report in the *Shrewsbury Chronicle* of the following Friday included a description of the new cemetery in a florid style typical of the time:

> In the alterations of the surface which were thought necessary, the natural features of the ground, and that adjoining have guided the artist, and consequently the whole wears an aspect the reverse of artificial. The area is apportioned for church and dissenters in the proportion of 15 to 4½ acres, the development being indicated by a white paved line and stone markers. The central and lower part of the consecrated ground is laid out to form a great circle of 4 acres, which is called 'The Great Grave Circle'. The walks which are 10 feet in width, traverse the general area, dividing the surface into convenient compartments. The cemetery is extensively planted with shrubs and trees; the yew, cypress, and cedar amongst the evergreens predominating. The long straight walks on the two boundaries are planted with limes, to form shady avenues. In planting, the object has been not so much to form an ornamental shrubbery as to procure shade in a situation so peculiarly exposed to the sun in hot weather, and break up the large surface into comparatively private and secluded sections, and to preserve solemnity without gloominess. As the plants grow and the graves increase the undergrowth will of course disappear, and the trees of forest dimensions will alone remain to spread abroad over the silent tombs their genial arms.

At their meeting on 5 December 1856 the Board expressed its warm approval of the arrangements for the consecration, and it was reported that the first burial in the new cemetery grounds had taken place on that same day. The burial was that of **Gabriel Swallow (45)** a 67-year-old gamekeeper from Castle Foregate. He was buried (for no apparently obvious reason) approximately half way along the western boundary of the Cemetery, near to the boundary path and was followed within a matter of days by **George Rodwell (45)** a 50-year-old book-binder, and a two-year-old child by the name of **Robert Evans (125)**. The Burial Board continued to manage the Cemetery until 1909 when, with the passing of the Shrewsbury Corporation Act, responsibility was formally passed to the Borough Council.

The indescribable carnage of the First World War and its impact 'back home' led to a significant change in people's attitude to death and burial. What has been described as the 'Victorian celebration of death', involved much pomp, ceremony and ostentation, even for the most humble funeral. Memorials in churchyards and cemeteries were often large and flamboyant and inscriptions florid and detailed. The slaughter of millions on the battlefields of Europe, however, left scarcely a family in the country unaffected and led, almost inevitably, to a major shift in funeral and burial customs. In particular, the military cemeteries which

A Shrewsbury Burial Board marker stone sprang up near the battlefields, *situated near the original cemetery entrance* and also here in Britain, were seen as a fitting memorial to the 'lost generation'. The sight of row upon row of neat white gravestones with simple inscriptions imprinted itself on the national consciousness, and cemeteries in Britain were never to be the same again.

In Shrewsbury, the Cemetery was becoming filled close to its capacity and plans were made for an extension from the west boundary up to the new by-pass, which had been opened by the Princess Royal on 23 May 1933. This extension was consecrated in October 1939, and the style of memorial in the two sections neatly exemplifies the changes which gradually evolved in the aftermath of the Great War. Later, at the outset of the Second World War, when fear of a German invasion was at its height, a huge range of 'home defences' were rapidly erected at strategic points across the country. In Shrewsbury Cemetery a 'spigot' mortar base was erected to cover the railway line in case an enemy tank used a railway line to attack the town. The spigot was a fairly crude weapon used by the Home Guard for anti-personnel and anti-tank action. Thankfully, however, it was never to see action.

Since then the Cemetery has been extended twice more (in 1974 and 1991), taking up the space between the old southern boundary and the railway line to

A general view of the cemetery

Welshpool. Today, unlike many of its contemporaries, Shrewsbury Cemetery is well maintained, making easy access to even the oldest burial plots still possible. Its aspect remains 'the reverse of artificial' and its trees still 'spread their genial arms abroad over the silent tombs'.

2 MAYORAL TALES

Perhaps not surprisingly, many of Shrewsbury's past mayors (at least 48) have been laid to rest in the General Cemetery. With only a few exceptions, all served their town and fellow townspeople to the best of their ability, carrying out their mayoral duties with dignity and probity. The stories of some of them, their achievements, and sometimes their weaknesses, will I hope serve as a suitable memorial to them all.

John Loxdale (181) (Conservative; 1840–1, 1858–9 and 1872–3) came from a family with a strong history of service in the legal profession and also a tradition of civic service. His father, Joseph, had been mayor in 1797, his eldest brother, also Joseph, was mayor in 1830, while another brother, James, was Town Clerk up to the 1834 Municipal Reform Act. The Act, however, displaced him and led to a controversial compensation case which cost the Council dearly. John helped his brother, seeking to vindicate him of exaggerated criticism in the local press. This led to one writer, in a political song, referring to the family's involvement by calling them the 'host of brazen Lox'.

John Loxdale followed the family tradition and became a solicitor, with offices in College Hill. He followed his father as Clerk of the Peace for the Borough in 1833, retiring in 1872. In this capacity he was head legal officer to the county magistrates, who not only tried summary crimes, but also, in the days before the advent of County Councils, ordered and financed major public works of road and bridge building. In 1839, when the magistrates formed a Finance Committee, he was not, as was the usual practice, given the post of Secretary. This led Loxdale to file a legal challenge, claiming the right to such appointment. A ruling given by the Solicitor-General, however, went against him and ruled that such appointments may be customary but were not 'as of right'. He was nevertheless appointed as Secretary to the Committee but with no remuneration. As in the case of his brother, the political knives of his opponents came out and accusations were made that he was seeking to profit unfairly from his position.

His three mayoralties were not particularly eventful but in 1841 he was to play a role which may well have had far-reaching effects in the national politics of this country. Loxdale was Returning Officer in the General Election of that year when Benjamin Disraeli became MP for Shrewsbury. During the campaigning, the Liberal party publicised the fact that Disraeli had debts of £22,000 (approximately £6 million today). 'Honest electors of Shrewsbury! Would you be represented by such a man?' they asked. The Liberal candidate Sir William Yardley even challenged 'Dizzy' to a duel on the matter. Hearing this, Loxdale called the future Prime Minister to his College Hill home and kept him amiably detained behind locked doors, thus calming him down and forestalling the duel. Had he not done so, the course of British politics may have taken a very different line.

John married his first cousin, Anne Loxdale, and they had three sons and a daughter. One of his sons, Geoffrey, was at the centre of a major scandal at Shrewsbury School in 1874. The headmaster, **Revd H.W. Moss (198)**, allegedly gave him 88 lashes till he bled, as punishment for having ale in his study. This was harsh treatment, even by Victorian standards, and it led to an inquiry by the governors and a parliamentary debate in which the Home Secretary referred to it as 'needlessly excessive' and beyond the legal limit of 60 lashes. However, due to certain contradictions in reports of the incident, the case against Moss could not be proved and he continued his career. When he retired in 1908, he had been headmaster for 42 years.

John Loxdale died on 27 March 1885 at the age of 85.

William James Clement (102) (Liberal 1862–3) was born in 1802 into a well-known medical family. He was educated at Shrewsbury School and then trained as a surgeon. After qualifying, he went into practice with his father and cousin before seeking a post at the Royal Salop Infirmary. His career there came to an abrupt end, however, when several local Tory gentlemen — aware that he was active in local politics as a Whig — signed an unofficial declaration never to consult him or recommend him for a post at the hospital. Clement therefore resumed his work in private practice.

He was an expert writer on medical subjects, publishing *Observations on Surgery and Pathology* in 1832, followed by a two-volume *Physiology of the Nervous and Vascular Systems*. He also contributed numerous papers to leading medical journals. He was later to decline both a baronetcy and a knighthood.

He became best known, however, for his work amongst the poor living in the slum areas of Shrewsbury. He steadfastly refused payment when treating them. In 1853 he was the founder of the Salopian Society for the Improvement of the Industrial Classes, a philanthropic group which raised money to provide proper health services for Shrewsbury's poor and needy. He also argued passionately in the Town Council for the setting up of a Public Health Inquiry into the town's slum conditions. Nye Bevan, Minister of Health when the NHS was founded in 1948, wrote in his book *The Promised Land*: 'Dr Clement was a founder of the principles on which the National Health Service was established.'

William Clement by W.W. Scott

Clement served the town of his birth as a Liberal councillor, Mayor and MP (twice elected in 1865 and 1868). In 1864, he was presented with a magnificent Epergne table centre piece by Shrewsbury Council and its people. Said to be one of the finest examples of Victorian silverware and weighing some 875 ounces, it was called the 'Silver Sabrina'. When the effects of Dr Clement's grand-daughter, Miss T.M.M. Clement of Gateway House in Castle Street, came up for sale in 1960 it was bought in auction for £350 by Frank Painter of the Service Garage, Ditherington. He then offered it to the Borough Council for the same price. They however declined, saying the price was beyond their means. It was later put up for sale by a London firm of valuers and fetched £25,000! The piece is now believed to be in Australia and valued at £75,000. It depicts Clement both as a Mayor, with ceremonial attendants, and as a doctor nursing a child.

A permanent memorial of Dr Clement's term as Mayor is the present chain of office, which he provided, at his own expense, in honour of the Prince of Wales' (later King Edward VII) wedding on 10 March 1863. The pendant, which has a representation of his old school, is suspended from a link displaying his personal coat of arms. One of its allegorical chain-links represents medical science, and shows his own name with that of Darwin.

Dr Clement died in 1870, aged 68. In 1873, a memorial obelisk with drinking fountain and lead cups was erected in the forecourt of Shrewsbury railway station. It stood there until 1897, when it was removed to a central position in The Dingle. Some years later, however, it was moved again to a much less obvious position among a group of trees at the corner of Victoria Avenue and St Julian Friars. Happily, in 2004, this memorial to the life and

The William Clement memorial obelisk

Thomas Southam by W.W. Ouless

work of Dr William Clement was fully renovated and restored. The inscription on the memorial reads: 'erected by his friends and fellow townsmen in grateful recognition of his enlightened public spirit, consummate professional skill and active private benevolence.' Two portraits of him can be found in Rowley's House Museum, Shrewsbury, both painted in the late 1830s, one by Philip Corbet and the other by William Scott. The latter hung originally in the splendid Victorian boardroom of the old RSI (Royal Salop Infirmary), behind St Mary's church. Clement's obituary in the *British Medical Journal* lists, at some length, his many achievements and qualities. It also describes him as having 'highly cultivated literary tastes', and being on 'terms of intimacy' with, amongst others, Charles Dickens.

Thomas Southam (22) (Conservative 1865–5, 1871–2 and 1884–6), besides being elected Mayor of Shrewsbury on three separate occasions — a rare but not unique achievement — served on the Town Council for a total of 44 years. In a speech of tribute to him, Alderman W.L. Browne said that to tell his life story was like telling Shrewsbury's story during the same period. Besides his service on the Council, he was a long-serving borough magistrate, a county magistrate, director of Shrewsbury workhouse and vice-chairman of the Atcham Poor Law Union. He also became a life-long Alderman of the town.

During his three terms as Mayor, many of the 'live' issues of the day in Shrewsbury came to the fore. These included street lighting, the revival of the old Shropshire and Potteries railway and its Abbey Foregate station, the expansion of the town's main railway station, the establishment of a 'new' market hall, a sewerage system for the town, the formation of a Smithfield (or 'dead meat') market and the conversion of the old Shrewsbury School buildings to a library and museum. His mayoralties were also not without controversy and in 1860 he sued a fellow Tory councillor over allegations of a fraudulent nomination to the Council (see John Frail below).

It is perhaps in his role as a local businessman, however, that he made the biggest impact. His father was a corn merchant from Bridgnorth (who later moved to Shrewsbury) and young Thomas began his career as a counter clerk for another merchant in the town. He clearly harboured greater ambitions, however, and in 1842 he set up his own business as a wine and ale merchant in Wyle Cop. By dint of his business acumen and dedication, the company gradually grew and flourished, so that by 1886 it had its own brewery, known as the Old Salop Brewery, in Chester Street (where the Gateway Centre now stands). A branch in Ludlow followed, and by 1900 the company owned 20 public houses in the Shrewsbury area and had branched out with the purchase of the Castle Mineral Water factories. It imported wine from France via Liverpool,

Thomas Southam's Brewery in Chester Street c.1914

and owned several of its own recipes including a variety of champagne and a 'Shropshire Liqueur'. The business continued to thrive and was eventually bought by Threlfall's (now part of Greenall Whitley) in 1967.

Thomas Southam died on 31 December 1895 at the age of 77, but until recently his memory lived on as he could be seen in his full mayoral robes on the inn sign of the Proud Salopian in Smithfield Road. The pub had previously been a Southam's house. Sadly both the name and the sign have now disappeared.

Perhaps the most colourful of all Shrewsbury's past mayors is **John Frail (182)** (Conservative 1878–9). Frail was born in 1804 and came from humble origins. He left school at 13, barely literate. He was appointed to a local barber, J.C. Nightingale, but absconded and spent more than two years performing with an acting troupe in Lancashire and Cheshire. However, Mr Nightingale reclaimed him after watching his show and he continued his apprenticeship. He later set up his own barber's shop in Shoplatch but retired in 1849 to concentrate on his other great interest — the Turf.

He had been a gambler for some time and learnt many of the 'tricks of the trade' from his friend 'Mad' Jack Mytton (1796–1834). In 1843 he became Clerk of the Course for Shrewsbury Racecourse in Monkmoor. There, he set about revitalising the business with a series of innovations. He altered the calendar of meetings, enlarged the race paddocks, introduced handicapping and race-trains and extended ownership by increased share-holding. As a result, patronage of the Course by the aristocracy increased and the races attracted more entries.

Not content however with local success, Frail went on to make his mark nationally in the racing world: he took a lease of Ludlow racecourse and became Clerk at Northampton, Huntingdon, Windsor and Manchester. In each case he repeated his innovations with continuing success. Until 1876, he was also Director of Bristol racecourse and when the 1873 season opened with a visit by the Prince of Wales (later Edward VII), he amused the royal guest by concluding a speech in hoping 'that the Prince might live long and prosper and that his dynasty might survive all Radicals, Fenians and revolutionary thieves for a thousand years.' His reputation even spread abroad, and in 1865 the French Emperor, Napolean III, invited him to start the equivalent of the English Derby at Versailles, an offer he declined.

Frail's energetic and abrasive approach to life led to the occasional dispute. On one occasion he argued over the ownership of a racehorse with Dr William Palmer. When Palmer threatened murder, Frail was forced to lock himself in his lodgings to forestall a possible attack. Later, he was a witness against Palmer at the celebrated Rugeley poisonings trial, which resulted in the Doctor's execution by hanging.

Frail was also a very active electioneer (the primary reason for his recent inclusion in the *Dictionary of National Biography*) and in 1839 he was Tory agent at the General Election in Ludlow. As was common at the time, the election was clearly corrupt on both sides (Frail himself gave bribes of up to £300) and an opponent accused him in the Press of sending 'foreign blackguards' — from Shrewsbury — to coerce voters in Ludlow. He also became the party's agent at successive elections in Shrewsbury. When acting for Sir Richard Jenkins in 1837, he was kidnapped in Claremont by thugs hired by his opponent; they planned to throw him into the Severn and he was only saved when an old lady reported the matter to the authorities!

Frail was elected councillor for Welsh Ward in Shrewsbury in 1855, and in 1859 was accused of corruption. In the previous year's municipal elections, he and **George Eddowes (182)** (mayor of Shrewsbury 1882–3, see below) distributed ballot papers at an inn, giving, it was alleged, 30 shillings to anyone who would vote for them. To tempt prospective supporters to come forward, they had with them a bowlful of silver coins and another of gold. John Watton, an ex-mayor, brought a suit against them at the town's assizes. The case, however, was thrown out. In 1860 Frail was sued by Thomas Southam for assault. Southam claimed he had been verbally abused by Frail over a minor error on a Council nomination and that Frail had threatened to beat him up and libellously accused him of having stolen money from a past employer. Frail was fined £3 and bound over to keep the peace. Over time his reputation and prestige in the town recovered. In 1865 he re-entered the Council and in 1878 was elected mayor. However, in March of the following year, he became the seventh and last mayor of Shrewsbury to die in office.

Thomas Corbett (21) (Independent 1906–7) was a founder member of Salop County Council in 1889, sitting for the Ditherington ward. He entered Borough politics when he was elected councillor for Coton Hill ward in 1904, and was an Alderman from 1910 until his death in 1917 at the age of 74.

It is in his role as a businessman and inventor, however, that the greatest interest lies. His father, Samuel Corbett, was a master of Park Street Ironworks in Wellington. After initially working in his father's firm, Thomas came to Shrewsbury in 1863 as implements agent and works manager to Samuelson and Co of the Perseverance Ironworks in St Michael's Street, whose main products were cheese presses and agricultural implements. When the owner of the Company retired the following year, Thomas Corbett, and a partner by the name of Chipchase, bought the firm. The works expanded to become the largest of its kind in the West Midlands and Corbett's creativeness and penchant for invention came to the fore.

In 1867 he patented a combined winnowing, elevating and weighing machine for preparing harvested corn. Known as the Eclipse, it won first prize in that

The Exors. of the late
THOMAS CORBETT,
Executors S. E. Corbett, E. E. Dawson, H. H .Humphries.
PERSEVERANCE IRON WORKS, SHREWSBURY,
HOLD MORE THAN 800 R.A.S.E. and other FIRST PRIZES,
GOLD and SILVER MEDALS, etc., for Superior and Practicable Manufactures.

All Corbett's
Manufactures
are special
Favourites
Everywhere
and are
Guaranteed
to work
Satisfactorily.

Makers of
Corn & Seed
Dressing
Machines,
Seed Drills,
Curd Mills,
Cheese Presses,
Ploughs,
Horse Hoes,
Food
Preparing
Machinery,
etc.

The Perseverance Implement Works.
LISTS AND PRICES ON APPLICATION.
Telegrams—" CORBETT SHREWSBURY."   Telephone **117**

S. EDWIN CORBETT'S
RETAIL IMPLEMENT WAREHOUSE
(Opposite Railway Station)

Contains
one of the
Largest
and
most
up-to-date
Collections of
Agricultural
Implements
etc.,
in Great
Britain.

Can
supply
all Leading
Makers'
Machines
and
Implements.

Wearing
Parts
for the
Leading
Harvesting
Machines,
Ploughs,
etc.

Sole Agents
for District
for
the Famous
Massey Harris
Binders,
etc.

Advertisement for products of Corbett's Perseverance Ironworks

year's Royal Show. The machine was in great demand and was even operated personally by the Prince of Wales at the 1872 Paris Exhibition. Later, he produced the horse-drawn Plane Binder which could bale sheaves of corn as quickly as they were mown. In 1884 came the Champion Digger, a strong light plough capable of being drawn by three horses, less than half the number in a typical plough-team of the time.

Corbett exhibited his machines at every Royal Show between 1867 and 1914, the last one being held at Shrewsbury when he was presented to the visiting King George V. He did not restrict

The Ironworks after a disastrous fire on the morning of 20 November 1905

20

himself to his native country however, he also exhibited in Paris, Brussels and Amsterdam and was presented to the kings of Belgium and Holland. Corbett was even created a Baron of the Dutch kingdom though, modestly, he never used the title in England. Over the years, his firm won over 1,000 prizes, medals and diplomas, and he was a member of the Royal Agricultural Societies of England and Holland as well as the Italian Industrial and Scientific Society, who awarded him their medal of honour. In Shrewsbury he was a founder member of the Shropshire and West Midlands Agricultural Society, of which he became Secretary, and helped promote the first 'West Mid' Show in 1876.

Corbett used his many journeys abroad to promote his products and, whenever possible, to see them in use. In return, he would often bring back ideas for adapting his products to suit the conditions in which they were used in. He made two round-the-world trips, and in 1905 visited the major Boer War battle-sites in South Africa.

Back home, his works were damaged by a major fire in 1905, which could have wrecked the business had it not missed the pattern shop where the designs of all his inventions were held. While salvaging among the ruins, Corbett narrowly escaped death when a wall collapsed next to him. The firm continued to operate until the 1920s, when increasing farm mechanisation and cheaper imported machinery led to its demise. The buildings are now occupied by the Morris Lubricants.

Morris Lubricants in the refurbished Ironworks buildings

21

The ancestry of **Thomas Pace (27)** (Liberal 1922–3) has been traced back to Italian immigrants who lived in London around 1380. The family first came to Shropshire, as farmers, in the early 1600s. They were said to be poor and illiterate.

Thomas Pace himself, however, became the archetypal 'self made man'. He was born in 1856 at Brierley Hill, one of eight children of a farm labourer who had just moved from Stockton near Bridgnorth in the hope of finding better work. Within weeks his hopes were dashed by a major strike accompanied by shut-outs at local mines. As a result, he returned to Stockton, where Thomas began work on a farm, at the age of nine, for 2 shillings a week.

His family later moved to Madeley where Thomas worked hard at his education and literacy. He then entered the building trade as a bricklayer's apprentice in Crewe, and came to Shrewsbury in 1874 where he worked for Treasure's, a local building firm. He quickly rose to the position of foreman, and in 1888 left to set up his own business in Greenfields Street, later moving to Coton Hill before retiring in 1926. The firm was responsible for many public buildings in Shrewsbury, including the Shirehall in The Square, demolished in 1889 after a fire; the Borough Police Station in Swan Hill; the St Michael's Street and Lancastrian Schools; three Methodist chapels and Coton Hill Congregational chapel (where he was Deacon).

The firm also built over 700 houses and was almost totally responsible for developing the Greenfields area to the north of the town, as well as much development in the Coleham and Kingsland areas.

Pace was elected councillor for Coton Hill ward in 1894 and sat as Alderman from 1920 to 1932. He also stood as Liberal candidate in the 1910 General Election and is said to have spent the entire week before Polling Day canvassing on a bicycle! Ultimately, he was a close runner-up to the sitting MP, Sir Clement Hill. In the Council, he was a firm supporter of slum clearance and used his experience and knowledge of building matters to good effect in debates on public works. One example was his insistence that the Council lay water-pipes under pavements instead of roads where traffic pressure could crack them. In 1921, when the Council faced a housing shortage of crisis proportions, he came up with a plan to cut the costs of house building. In his estimation, this could be done for £700, with innovations such as single pane windows and flat, concrete roofs. He also suggested raising money by offering plots of land to people who wished to build their own homes. During his mayoralty, a tender was finally accepted for re-building the English Bridge, and he also formally opened Port Hill suspension bridge.

Pace was also one of the first motorists in Shrewsbury and one of the first to own several cars at the same time. His driving career, however, ended in tragedy. After 30 years' motoring, he was involved in a terrible accident in

Barker Street in 1928. He was picking up his wife at the time in a new car, with which he was barely familiar. On re-starting, without warning he ran into a queue of people entering a bus, injuring several and killing one 51 year old woman. As a result, he was fined £10 and banned from driving for seven years. He did not live to see the end of his ban and died aged 78 in 1933.

It is surely rare for someone from a show business background to enter politics and then be elected Mayor. This is the path, however, trodden by **Robert Bates Maddison (117)** (Conservative 1923–25). He was born at Blaydon, County Durham on 7 July 1862. His family later moved to Sunderland and it was there that the young Robert Maddison learnt to sing and took part in amateur performances. He joined the famous D'Oyly Carte Opera Company in 1884 and toured with them. In 1899 he married Emma Hall, a soprano, who often partnered him on stage; they had one son, Gerald. Mrs Maddison died in 1935 and two years later he married Mrs Peggy Dentith of Preston.

In the summer of 1914, he and his first wife were taking part in an elaborate operetta, *The Venetians*, which toured various European cities. In July, however, the German invasion of Belgium put paid to the whole project and he was forced to take the quick decision to return to England and set up in business. Later that year, he bought the County Theatre in Shoplatch, Shrewsbury and the George Hotel next door (since demolished). As owner, and some-time manager, he staged many fine classical operettas there and continued to sing on stage himself until the age of 70.

What was once the County Theatre in Shoplatch

The interior of the County Theatre in Shoplatch, which subsequently became a cinema until wrecked by a fire in 1945

Mr Maddison was elected councillor for Castle ward in 1920 and became an Alderman in 1930. In 1924, when he was Mayor of Shrewsbury, an unsavoury incident at the theatre led to a court appearance for the town's 'first citizen'. Two members of the audience were found to be sitting in the wrong seats and when they refused to leave, a policeman was called. When they continued to hold their ground, Maddison pulled one of them, Alfred Hawkins, out of his seat, taunting and berating him. As it turned out, the men's tickets had been stamped with the wrong details and Hawkins received £25 from the Mayor after suing him for slander.

His mayoralty came in the depression years between the Wars when unemployment and housing shortages were the major problems facing the town. In Ditherington and Coton Hill over 100 houses were planned but not completed by the end of his term. There was extensive over-crowding and tenants were unable to afford the charges needed to pay off the building costs. Some of the more extreme cases of hardship uncovered included a family of six sleeping in a disused chapel; unofficial squatting in council houses in Sultan Road, which were newly built but still empty; and a family who lived alternately in a fish shop and a van. Some relief came, however, in March 1925 when the 56 acre site of Monkmoor Racecourse was purchased for house-building.

Maddison was also a keen motorist and in March 1942 only narrowly escaped death when he accidentally drove his car into the overhang of a parked lorry in the town centre, smashing the car's windscreen and leaving him with severe facial injuries. He died on 26 April 1949 aged 86 and one of the bequests in his will was to the Actors' and Music Hall Benevolent Fund.

Mrs Marion Wallace Cock (133) (Conservative 1934–35), whose ashes were scattered on the family grave in the Cemetery, was born at Valparaiso, Chile in 1883, the daughter of William Scott, a Scotsman who was in the import and export business. Happily he lived long enough to see his daughter achieve the distinction of becoming Shrewsbury's first woman Mayor. Through her American mother, Emma Holmar, she was descended from one of the Pilgrim Fathers who settled in the new continent in 1620. When she was two years old the family moved to Scotland, and she was educated initially in Edinburgh and then Switzerland. In 1904 she married James Cock, brother of a school friend and head of the Shrewsbury Tannery of James Cock and Sons in Barker Street.

It was in the last decade before the First World War that she developed an interest in local politics and public life. This was at a time when the very idea of a married lady becoming involved in such matters was still viewed with scorn and even ridicule. She was an active — though not militant — supporter of the suffragette movement, and in 1910 became Shropshire's first County Commissioner for Girl Guides. During the 1914–18 War she was a nurse at the military hospital established at Oakley Grange in Belle Vue.

In 1920 her husband died in a shooting accident and she was left to bring up six children on her own. Against much advice, she took over her husband's tannery becoming, it was said, the only woman in such a position in the country. She continued to run the business until two years before her death. She did not, however, let her business commitments interfere with her activities in local politics. In 1934 she became the last Mayor of Shrewsbury to have to meet her own expenses, and it was largely through her efforts that future Mayors received an allowance from the Council.

On her election as Mayor she somewhat optimistically proposed that Shrewsbury have its own civic airport: 'I feel we should lose no time before another quarter of a century has passed', she said, 'the town that does not have its airport will be of no account. We must prepare ... for the era of air transport.' Sadly, suggested sites were all rejected, the government refused financial aid and the project fell through. During her time as Mayor, however, she opened the Shelton water works, received a public visit by the Duke of York (later King George VI) and presented a badge of office for future Deputy Mayors. She later became the first female recipient of the freedom of Shrewsbury.

The opening of Shrewsbury's new waterworks in July 1935. Mrs Marion Cock is holding the bunch of flowers and talking to the Revd. E.M. Darling. To her right is Lady Bridgeman, who performed the opening ceremony, and the Town Clerk, Mr Prideux. On the far left is the next mayor, Mr Charles Beddard

Mrs Cock died on 19 December 1958 aged 75, but not before seeing her daughter-in-law, Mrs Eleanor Mary Cock, become Shrewsbury's second female Mayor in 1956.

Charles Beddard (117) (Conservative 1935–37) was born at Sedgeley, Staffordshire, in 1872. After leaving school, he entered the butchery trade and became a bacon curer in Bilston and Wolverhampton before moving to Shrewsbury in 1912. His first shop in the town was on Wyle Cop, though he moved to numbers 4 and 5 Mardol in 1915. The shop continued to be run by his family until it was sold in 1963. For many years he was president of the local Master Butchers' Association.

During the 1914–18 War he pleaded for the cause of his fellow traders during the labour shortage and business difficulties caused by conscription. At one point, whilst arguing his cause, he warned the then Mayor — **Sir Samuel Morris (132)** — 'It is a very serious thing for the trade, but if you are going to starve the people at home, then those who are fighting for us will not think much of you.'

Beddard's short, stout figure was a familiar sight at regional livestock markets and he is known to have on occasions taken home pigs he had bought in his car! From 1928 he was chairman of the Council's Water Committee and must take much of the credit for the erection of the town's present water works. In 1929 he put in motion an eight-year-long construction project on the water supply system, and in March 1931 shocked the Council by unveiling plans for a completely new water works to be built on a seven-acre site at Shelton and costing £17,000. The existing Coton Hill works were too weak to supply the population of the day; the new works had to be capable of pumping 1,400,000 gallons of water a day.

'Shrewsbury has plenty of water but no facilities for putting it in the proper place', he said. A Loughborough firm was contracted to build the works and it was proposed that 80% of the labour be selected from local unemployed men, at a time of very high unemployment. The Shelton water works were opened in 1935 and the cylindrical water tower, which is still a prominent landmark, became known locally as 'Charlie Beddard's pork pie'.

Charles Beddard died at his flat above the Plough Inn on The Square on 10 February 1941, aged 68. In 1970 his daughter, Miss Mary Beddard, presented to the Corporation a silver rose bowl which Shelton water works' consulting engineers had given her father as a memento of its opening.

Harry Steward (Plot 10) (Independent/Conservative 1938–45) was Mayor of Shrewsbury for a continuous period of seven years — the longest in the town's history. He was born on 18 August 1892 and educated at the Boys High School on Wyle Cop (now demolished) and at Wrekin College. There he distinguished himself as an athlete, winning prizes for sprinting, swimming and hurdling. He also played football and cricket for the College.

In the First World War he joined the 6th King's Shropshire Light Infantry (known as the 'Shrewsbury Pals' battalion because so many of its members were friends or relations of each other). He served on the western front, and in 1917 was commissioned and attached as Captain in the Cheshire Regiment. In October 1918 he won the Military Cross at the recapture of Menin. After the War he entered local politics and was elected borough councillor for Coton Hill ward, becoming an Alderman in 1939. He was also a county councillor for Kingsland ward from 1946.

His mayoralty might not have been so long but for the fact that the Second World War broke out during his first year in office. Contested political elections were suspended, so the popular Steward was re-elected six consecutive times. During the first month of the War 3,000 evacuees arrived in Shrewsbury from Merseyside, and homes had to be found for each of them. More than 13,000 air raid shelters were made ready for use, and the Council even set aside space in the cellars of the Market Hall and other public buildings. An Auxiliary Fire Service fleet was established, a salvage depot for scrap set up and unnecessary railings removed from all public buildings. The Mayor played a personal role

27

also: the warehouse of his grocery shop in Pride Hill was used as a scrap depository and he organised the local Boy Scouts (of whom he was District Commissioner) in running salvage collections.

'Dig for Victory' became a familiar slogan. Allotments were increasingly popular and, by the end of 1942, the Council had taken over some 2,000 plots. Good publicity and propaganda were achieved when the lawns of the Quarry were ploughed up to make kitchen gardens for the town's schools. To mark VE and VJ days he presented new links for the mayoral chain, and in 1945 received the OBE for his wartime duties.

Steward also sowed many of the seeds of Shrewsbury's present day 'twinning' with Zutphen in Holland. Links between the towns go back to 1585 and the death of Sir Philip Sidney (an old boy of Shrewsbury School) in helping to relieve the city from the Spaniards. As the town's Mayor, Steward appealed to the people of Shrewsbury for clothing, blankets, utensils, crockery and tools to be used in the post-war reconstruction of Zutphen. In 1946 he made a civic visit and was made an 'honorary citizen' of the Dutch city.

Harry Steward was heavily involved in the Boy Scout movement, being Master of St Mary's Troop and District Commissioner from 1933 to 1953. He was awarded the Scout Medal of Merit, with a 'national service' bar for his involvement in wartime salvage and fundraising efforts. In his mayoral election speech, he said: 'I belong to a movement that is divided into three parts, the Wolf Cubs, whose motto is "I will do my best", the Scouts whose motto is "Be prepared" and the Rover Scouts whose motto is "Service". I do not think that any Mayor could start his year of office with a better motto than ... "I will do my best to be prepared for service"!'

On 13 December 1954, at the age of 62, he had a heart attack whilst at a Borough Council meeting in Shrewsbury Castle. Fellow councillors and Council officials went to his aid and he was taken to the Mayor's parlour and then the Royal Salop Infirmary, but was found to be dead on arrival.

Two other past Mayors of Shrewsbury are worthy of note here. The story of **Samuel Pountney Smith (190),** architect of the Cemetery buildings, can be found in chapter one and **John Milns West (162),** master of Shrewsbury School, is covered in chapter nine.

3   MINISTERS, MISSIONARIES AND MORE

For some years prior to 1854, Welsh Calvinistic Methodists in Shrewsbury had been meeting in a chapel in Hills Lane. Services were held in Welsh however, and there was no provision at all for those members who spoke only English. Whilst they were a significant minority, there was too few of them to form a separate congregation.

In 1854, the Revd Ebenezer Williams became Pastor at Hills Lane. However, his wife did not speak Welsh and petitioned successfully to be allowed to run a Bible Class in English. Over time, the Class developed into a Sunday School and became the origin of what became known as the 'English cause' in Shrewsbury. On the death of the Revd Williams in 1858, English services were initially suspended, but were re-started later by his widow. The venture flourished, and in 1861 Mrs Williams appealed for donations; with the £30 raised, she bought church furniture and a communion plate, which allowed them to hold services in rented premises in Claremont Hill. The **Revd W. Hinton Jones (17)** was one of the ministers who occasionally officiated for them there. Anxious, however, to have a chapel of their own, they purchased a site in Frankwell Quay where they opened a brand new chapel in April 1865, the building being designed by the Borough Engineer, **Thomas Tisdale (57)**. The chapel itself was on the first floor, approached by a flight of steps at the front of the building. The ground floor was occupied by a Sunday School and nearby was a schoolmistress's house. The Revd Hinton Jones was appointed as its first Pastor and continued in that position for the next 27 years. In 1869 he married, and his wife became an active supporter and member of the church.

The site of the chapel was not without problems, however, being below the flood level of the nearby River Severn. It was often surrounded by water and on one occasion members of the congregation could only attend their anniversary service by walking along planks; on another occasion, services had to be completely abandoned. In 1891 Mr Hinton Jones resigned and a joint Pastorate was established with the Hills Lane church. By the early years of the 20th century, it had become clear that the site in Frankwell was too small. This, in addition perhaps to the regular flooding problems, prompted

The old Calvinistic Methodist chapel in Frankwell
— in 2006 occupied by a tyre company

the members to set out on an ambitious project to establish new and extensive premises in a more central position. They acquired a property at Belmont Bank for £2,320 and plans were drawn up by a Mr Dickins Lewis for a building which was not so much a chapel as a lecture hall with classrooms. It was built for a further cost of £1,190 in 1904, the 50th anniversary of the establishment of the church.

The old chapel in Frankwell continued in use as a mission church until 1909 when the building was sold. Today (2006) it is occupied by a tyre company and is still subject to occasional flooding. Mr Hinton Jones died on 19 May 1899 aged 62 and so did not live to see the developments in Belmont. His gravestone in Shrewsbury cemetery records his service at the Frankwell chapel and describes him as 'an original thinker, an eloquent preacher and a devoted minister of Jesus Christ.'

On 5 March 1865, a new English Presbyterian church in Shrewsbury held its first service in the Music Hall. At the close of the service, a committee was formed to oversee the development of the new church. A month later, services began to be held in the Long Room of the Lion Hotel at the top of Wyle Cop and a Sunday School also began.

The congregation felt the need, however, for a permanent chapel of their own. After a possible site in Dogpole was rejected, they decided on one in Castle Gates immediately outside the entrance to the castle and appointed Mr Robert C. Bennett of Weymouth as architect. The foundation stone was laid on 18 January 1870 and the building opened for services on 16 December of the same year. The total cost of the project was some £3,500 and the result was a tall elegant building in the Norman style. It was dedicated to St Nicholas for the reason that it stood on the site of an old chapel of St Nicholas which was used by

The old Presbyterian chapel in Castle Gates

retainers of the castle. Today the building still stands proudly opposite the Library and old School buildings, though it is now in use as commercial offices.

Its first minister, the Revd James Cree, resigned to work in New Zealand and his successor was the **Revd John Vance Moore (42)**. Moore was the eldest son of the Revd A.F. Moore, a minister in Castle Blaney in County Monaghan. He was educated initially by his father and then at Trinity College, Dublin. On 9 June 1874, he was inducted at Shrewsbury and was described as having, 'a bright and winsome personality and a ministry of great purpose.' Sadly, however, that promise was never to be realised as in the following year he was struck down tragically by scarlet fever at only 26 years of age. Although only recently settled in the town, he had already begun to make his influence felt and his premature death came as a great shock to all who knew him. His congregation and other friends erected a monument over his grave in the cemetery and placed a photograph of it in the vestry of the chapel.

St Nicholas' continued to be used for religious services up until 1975 when the congregation joined with the United Reformed Church next to the English Bridge.

Julia Bainbrigge Wightman (70) (née James) was born in 1815, the daughter of Lt Col James of Bath. She was of aristocratic descent and could trace her family line from King Edward III. In 1842, she married the **Revd Charles Edward Leopold Wightman (70),** vicar of St Alkmund's in Shrewsbury. He himself was the grandson of a Russian prince, his mother was a companion and friend of Princess Charlotte, and his three names were given by his three godparents , the Princess Charlotte, Edward Duke of Kent (father of Queen Victoria) and Prince Leopold of Belgium.

Julia's father was initially strongly opposed to the marriage, for two reasons. The first was that his daughter had always been a delicate child and he thought that the arduous tasks which fell to a clergyman's wife would be too much for her. The second was that he considered Charles too serious-minded for a girl so full of life and gaiety. Nevertheless, it was only when she became seriously ill as a result of her grief, that he withdrew his objections and, as their life together unfolded, it became clear that he could not have been more wrong in his concerns.

Charles Wightman had been educated at Lincoln College, Oxford, taking his BA in 1838. After a curacy in Saltford near Bristol, an arrangement was made with the Crown that his father should vacate his incumbency at St Alkmund's in favour of his son. Charles ministered in that parish for more than 52 years.

So it was at St Alkmund's vicarage, Shrewsbury, that Julia began her lifelong commitment to work amongst the poor and destitute. At a time when

St Alkmund's Vicarage, home of the Wightmans

The Wightmans

a woman's place was seen to be very firmly in the home, she would be out visiting in the working class districts of the town on five nights of the week, often until late in the evening. In 1858, one of the Borough magistrates was moved to comment that he had seen Mrs Wightman walking home at 10pm accompanied by the most notorious poacher in the neighbourhood. When a friend remarked to her that it must take great courage to be in the company of such rough men, she replied, 'No it does not, it requires love, and that's a thing few people possess for their poorer brothers and sisters; I cannot account for it, but I love them all with all my heart, and they know it.'

She concentrated her efforts initially on the area around Butcher Row, at the time a poverty-stricken area, squalid and vice-ridden. It was her experience there of the degradation which resulted from drunkenness, that led her to throw herself wholeheartedly into a campaign against it. It is said that one gentleman, on meeting Revd Wightman for the first time, said: 'Are you the Mr Wightman who ...' before floundering in confusion. The reply was: 'Yes, I am the Mr Wightman who is so proud to be known as the husband of Mrs Wightman.'

Never a supporter of temperance, she insisted at all times on total abstinence, reasoning that the only way to 'cure' a man of drunkenness was to completely remove the temptation. Her attitude and influence, however, were far from negative. Her aim always was to introduce self-respect and a fresh outlook on life. It was said of her work that 'many homes, once the abode of wretchedness, are now the dwellings of happiness and peace'. She also realised that time once spent in the public houses of the town had to be filled by other means and consequently established Bible Classes and night schools for working class men.

Her most significant and lasting impact, however, was achieved through her book *Haste to the Rescue*. Unable to find time to write a book from 'scratch', she instead put together a series of letters she had written to her sister and to a Miss Marsh. In them she described her work and her approach to the challenges she faced. The book had a huge and immediate impact. It sold phenomenally and circulated almost all over the world, was re-printed in America and ran to four editions in Dutch. In its introduction, she outlined her aims:

> This little book is written chiefly for the educated classes, and has one object – the stirring up of every heart to more earnest and prayerful effort to rescue those who are placed by God in a less favourable position, from the thraldome of THE ONE besetting temptation, which is to them the fruitful source of all other sin and sorrow, and by loving acts of sympathy and kindness to elevate them socially and morally.

As well as describing her work with individuals and groups, the book also contains some scathing criticism of Shrewsbury Show, which by the mid 19th century seems to have become little more than an excuse for drunkenness and disorder. She argued that this was to the detriment of families, saying: 'The truth is that love of money, not the love of the working class is at the root of the matter.' She went on to write that Show Monday was a harvest time, not for the shop-keepers but for the publicans.

After the great success of her first venture into print, other books were to follow with dramatic titles such as: *Annals of the Rescued*, *Arrest the Destroyer's March*, *More than Conqueror* and *The Church Militant and Triumphant*. Her writings played a significant part in a movement which led ultimately to the establishment of the Church of England Temperance Society. In his book *Lives Worth Living*, the Revd Charles Bullock compared their impact to that of *Uncle Tom's Cabin* in relation to the emancipation of slaves in America.

Mrs Wightman used the profits from the sale of *Haste to the Rescue* to fund probably her greatest philanthropic venture in the town. It had become clear that, if the benefits of the

The Wightmans' grave

work she had begun were to be sustained, something more than church services and Bible Classes was needed. Plans for a Working Men's Hall were hatched and she bought a suitable site (for £700) just off The Square in Princess Street — now occupied by the Jane Dyas shop. Ironically, the Fox Hotel stood on the site at the time — a notorious haunt of hard drinkers and felons.

The 'public house without a drink', as it became known, was a completely new idea for Shrewsbury and one of only a few in the country at that time. It was designed by John L. Randell of Shrewsbury and built by a Mr Treasure of Newport, Shropshire, for a total cost of £3,685 11s. A public appeal raised £2,244 9s and the balance was met personally by the Revd and Mrs Wightman. Some of the conditions laid down in the trust document describe its purpose and range of activities:

> The ground floor will contain baths for hot and cold water, rooms for night schools, a reading room, etc., library where papers and periodicals will be supplied, a room where Friendly Societies may transact business, instead of meeting in a public house, and a large common room to which a man may take a friend at any hour, a great boon especially on wet days, and where coffee, etc., will be supplied. On the first floor will be a lecture hall for the weekly meetings of our association.

The opening of the Working Men's Hall was a grand occasion. A procession of nearly 1,000 people, including a bishop, 80 clergymen and their wives, the mayor and corporation of Shrewsbury and Dr Kennedy, headmaster of Shrewsbury School made its way from St Alkmund's church to the splendid new building in Princess Street. At the head of the procession were two banners, one belonging to the Total Abstinence Society and the other the Diocesan church. A dense crowd lined the streets to see this impressive parade.

After a lifetime's work for the cause of abstinence, Mrs Wightman died on 14 January 1898. Her husband had pre-deceased her by three years. The day of her funeral was said to be exactly 40 years from the day her first convert signed the 'pledge'. The two are buried together at a spot in the Cemetery chosen by them together, just before the Revd Wightman's final illness.

Some of her many supporters and helpers are also buried with her in the Cemetery. From the outset, her aim had been to train members of her Society to assist in her 'great work' and among her most trusted helpers was **Henry Halford Powell (152)**. He had been one of the earliest members of her team and, as well as doing a considerable amount of visiting, he would, in Mrs Wightman's absence, take up to three meetings a week. During periods when she was incapacitated through illness, she would write letters from her sick bed to be read at meetings of her Society. Unknown to her, Powell carefully preserved many of these letters and shortly before his death in September 1873, he pointed to a drawer and whispered to Mrs Wightman, 'There is something there which belongs to you, or rather it is the property of our Society; some of your letters to us which have been kept safe.' A few days later, his widow sent a package to Mrs Wightman containing all the letters.

The letters were put together into a booklet of some 50 pages, entitled *Memorial Letters*. Mrs Wightman also compiled a touching memorial to her old friend and issued it, in the form of a pamphlet, to every member. Powell was only 45 when he died. His gravestone was erected by 'members and other friends' in 'grateful and loving remembrance of his valuable services in St Alkmund's Total Abstinence Society during 15 years.'

The gravestone of **Richard Stedman (90),** who died on 8 May 1859 aged 44, was also erected by his friends in the Society. He was clearly a much loved and respected member. In one of her letters included in her book *Haste to the Rescue*, Mrs Wightman recorded the effects of his last illness:

> I grieve to say poor Stedman broke a second blood-vessel the night before, after his return from the prayer-meeting. He ought not to have been with us at our tea party; but he looked so happy to be amongst us, we could not find it in our hearts to forbid his coming. His pale face quite upset me; and C. Thomas said, 'I can't look at him without getting my eyes full of tears.' He is now laid up in bed. I do not know how I shall bear to lose him.

After they had 'laid the body of our beloved brother to rest', Mrs Wightman recorded a further sad development: 'Darling little Dicky, Stedman's eldest boy, gradually faded away from the time of his father's death.'

The beneficial influence of the Wightmans was not restricted to their own parish and town. Several members of St Alkmund's church left to work as missionaries abroad during their time there. Amongst these was **Arthur Poole (43)** who had been brought up in the parish from early childhood and was to become the first Anglican Bishop of Japan. Mrs Wightman was able to attend his consecration at Lambeth on St Luke's Day 1883.

Poole, however, was to die less than two years later at the early age of 32. The Wightmans were staying at Barmouth at the time but Charles returned home to take his friend's funeral service. Later, the Wightmans were to be buried only a few yards away from him in Shrewsbury Cemetery.

4   RAILWAY TRAGEDIES

On 15 October 1907, just after 2am, a train derailed at speed just outside Shrewsbury railway station causing what the *Shrewsbury Chronicle* called, without exaggeration, 'one of the most terrible accidents of modern times.' That it followed on closely from two almost identical accidents at Salisbury and Grantham, only served to heighten its impact on the national consciousness.

The train involved was the 1.20am London and North Western mail train from Crewe to Shrewsbury, Hereford, Bristol and the West of England. It consisted of 15 'vehicles', including five passenger carriages carrying a relatively light passenger complement of around 70. The train left Crewe eight minutes late, but between Whitchurch and Shrewsbury the driver maintained an average of 60mph and regained five minutes. In order to enter Shrewsbury platform, the train had to take a tight curve of only 610ft radius, over which speed was restricted to 10mph. Two signal boxes controlled the approach to the station: Crewe Bank and Crewe Junction. When Crewe Bank 'offered' the train to the junction, it was accepted under the 'section clear but station blocked' signal, which meant that the Crewe Bank signalman must stop and caution the train. He therefore kept his signals at danger but, to his horror, saw the train run past his box — only 600 yards from the junction curve — at full speed, and realised that disaster was inevitable. He immediately sent the 'train running away on right lane' signal to the Crewe Junction box, but by the time the signalman there received it, the train was, in his own words, 'all across the junction.'

The engine travelled for 75 yards over the sleepers and ballast, before it was flung over on its side. The coaches piled up on the engine, tearing up two sets of rails for a distance of 140 yards. An eye-witness described the scene after the crash:

> Dreadful sights were seen on every hand. Here a dreadfully mutilated body was revealed, there sufferers were discovered hopelessly involved in the wreckage and imploring to be released. One by one the bodies were removed and ere long the parcels office on the island platform was converted into a gruesome and bloodstained mortuary.

The 1907 railway accident (PH/S/13/R/3)

Eighteen lives were lost: eleven passengers, the driver and fireman, two guards and three Post Office sorters; 33 others were listed as injured. Railway staff were joined by postal sorters from the nearby Castle Foregate office in the desperate rescue attempts that followed. The three Post Office sorters amongst the dead were all Shrewsbury men. **Stephen Crabtree Hodgson (192)**, **Henry Morris (186)** and **Leonard Denham Bradley (178)** were all buried in Shrewsbury Cemetery, as was one of the passengers, **Antonio Colombotti (51)** of Princess Street, Shrewsbury. Colombotti's body was later re-interred in his native Italy.

A special memorial service for the dead was held at St Chad's church on the following Sunday and the Mayor of Shrewsbury, **Thomas Corbett (21)** (see Chapter Two) opened a public appeal fund. Corbett had also personally visited the site of the disaster whilst rescue attempts were still underway. Post Office bosses made a written appeal to all Post Office employees in the UK, with individual subscriptions not to exceed 2s 6d. A simple brass tablet was erected in Shrewsbury main Post Office to the memory of Hodgson, Morris and Bradley. Today it stands in the reception area of the Castle Foregate sorting office. Stephen Hodgson left a widow and seven children, including a daughter born on the day he was laid to rest in Shrewsbury Cemetery. A

The wreckage of the 1907 railway accident
viewed across Shrewsbury's rooftops (PH/S/13/R/3)

separate fund was also established by the Post Office, devoted to the interests of the seven fatherless children.

A Board of Trade Enquiry began its work the day after the terrible accident. Relatives of four of the victims were represented by local solicitor, **John Bowdler (134)** (see Chapter Ten). To the relief of the families of the victims, the railway company accepted at the outset full responsibility for the accident. Much time was spent examining the backgrounds and characters of Driver Martin and Fireman Fletcher, who were in charge of the engine at the time and who both died in the accident. Fletcher, aged 29, was depicted as a man of a 'steady, sober and thrifty nature' and a strict teetotaller; he had never acted as Fireman for Martin before. Martin, however, had something of a chequered background and his record as a Driver was far from unblemished. He had 13 disciplinary entries against his name: five for absence without leave or missing his train, four for running past stations where he was due to stop, two for over-running signals on 'danger', one for dropping 17 minutes without cause and one for emitting black smoke at a station. In a masterpiece of understatement, the Inspecting Officer suggested that this indicated, 'to put it mildly, an occasional lack of attention on Martin's part to his duties.'

Martin, aged 52, was a large man of 14 stone and was said, from the condition of his kidneys, to be 'used to alcohol.' The Police Surgeon, Dr C.V. Bulstrode, however, confirmed that there was no evidence of alcohol in his stomach at the time of the accident. His turn of duty that day had not been a particularly arduous one. He, along with Fletcher, had had over 12 hours rest before coming on duty at 7.30pm the previous evening. Nevertheless, it

The crash site (PH/S/13/R/3)

was said that he had been out of bed for four of the previous six nights, and a number of retired enginemen gave evidence of the difficulties of getting proper sleep during day-time rests, and of personal experience of having fallen asleep for a few minutes whilst on the footplate. Over time, a general theory has become accepted that Martin must have dozed off, his hand still on the regulator handle. Fletcher would perhaps have been too busy filling the boiler and stoking his fire to have noticed this until any desperate attempts to remedy the situation had become futile. The full truth of what happened that fateful morning, however, may never be known.

News of the tragedy had an emotional impact on many people. Among them was a young lady by the name of **Gladys Mary Webb (15)** (see Chapter Six). She lived at the time with her family in Meole Brace and was still recovering from an attack of Grave's Disease, which was to affect her for much of her short life. She was a solitary and sensitive person, but at the age of 26 had already shown evidence of a natural gift for writing. On hearing of the accident, Mary was moved to write a compassionate poem which her brother,

Kenneth, subsequently found on her writing table. He was impressed with what he read and impulsively put the poem in his pocket. If published, he thought, it might give comfort and prompt help. Underlying his actions also was a conviction that his sister had an exceptional literary talent and, admiring her gift, he regretted that she tore up and burnt so many of her poems.

Memorial plaque in Shrewsbury Sorting Office to the three post office sorters killed in the 1907 accident

With an element of brotherly pride, he took Mary's 'railway poem' to the local newspaper offices. It was published on 18 October 1907 in the *Shrewsbury Chronicle*, alongside a report of the disaster. The poem begins:

> A night wind soughed around the speeding train
>   Unsatisfied, complaining,
> Demanding something – someone for its own;
> None heard, for sleep and laughter drowned its moan.
> 'Lamps lit, blinds down, what matter if 'tis raining?'
> In the foreboding wind the lights were straining ...

Although her work was published anonymously, Mary was appalled to see her poem — all five verses — in the newspaper. Her annoyance with her brother was tempered though when letters of appreciation began to pour in to the *Chronicle*'s offices. As a result, Kenneth noticed, Mary began to write with increasing confidence and so began a literary career during which she was to produce classic works such as *Gone to Earth*, *The Golden Arrow* and *Precious Bane*.

At least seven other deaths from railway accidents are recorded on gravestones in Shrewsbury Cemetery. **William James Morgan (172)** 'met his death by a casualty on a railway near Nuneaton', at the age of only 25 on 10 May 1858. **John Harris' (152)** grave is on the eastern edge of the 'great grave circle' in the centre of the Cemetery. His epitaph records that he died in December 1861 aged 86 and 'was for 44 years gardener at Lythwood Hall much respected by his employer'. His grandson, **Thomas Harris (152)**, is buried in the same grave; he was 'accidentally killed on the Railway' on 8 January 1863. A year earlier **Joseph Jobson (173)** of Shrewsbury had died, aged 57, 'from injuries in a collision on Shrewsbury and Hereford Railway.'

James Griffiths (57) had achieved the rank of Foreman on the railway at the relatively young age of 24. Sadly, at that age he was killed on 2 May 1871 crossing the line at Shrewsbury. His gravestone was erected by the 'Sick and Burial Society of the London and North Western Locomotive Department (Salop and Stafford Stations).' **John Cowdell (40)** also lost his life in a railway accident, on the Great Western Railway. He died aged 50 on 24 May 1883.

The circumstances of two railway deaths from the first half of the 20th century are worthy of record. **Walter Vaughan (184)**, a railway guard based at Shrewsbury who lived in Bynner Street, Belle Vue, lost his life at the Trent junction near Stafford on 17 May 1938 at the age of 52. The dreadful accident occurred when two London, Midland and Scottish Railway (LMS) goods trains collided and the brake van in which he was travelling was struck broadside on and carried 40 yards on the front of the engine of the other train until it eventually left the rails and ground to a halt. The two trains involved were the 9pm Burton to Swansea (pulling approximately 50 trucks) and the 10pm Birmingham to Manchester (consisting of 43 trucks). The Burton train was at a standstill on a loop line, waiting to be drawn into the yard, when it was hit in the rear by the Manchester train. The *Shrewsbury Chronicle* report describes how 'trucks and vans were piled on top of one another, wheels were torn from wagons, and the contents of vans strewn along the line.' Mr Vaughan had been a Company Sergeant Major in the St John Ambulance Brigade and was a leading figure in the local Railway Ambulance Corps. He had joined the LMS shortly before the First World War and during the War he served as a Sergeant in the Royal Marines, taking part in the Gallipoli campaign. He left a widow, four daughters and a son.

Ten years earlier, **William Henry Carter (207)** of Coton Mount, Shrewsbury had been a locomotive Fireman on the Great Western Railway. He was to die in a very different type of railway accident near to his home, at the Coton Hill goods yard. Carter, at the age of 28, was married with three children; he was the Fireman on a goods train which left Pontypool Road for Shrewsbury on 10 August 1928. It pulled up at Coton Hill next to a water column and he remained on the footplate to fill the boiler and put coal on the fire. Carter pulled a chain used to operate the filling mechanism and, when it snapped, fell eight feet on to the rail below. Colleagues carried him clear of the line and he was taken to Shrewsbury Station on a shunting engine, paralysed from the neck down. He never recovered. The Inquest jury expressed the view that the chain was badly worn and should have been replaced earlier. They saved their most scathing criticism, however, for the care he received after the accident, describing it as lamentable. A Dr Bridgman, in his evidence, stressed the need for extreme care when dealing with spinal injuries; lifting the victim's head could lead to instant death, he said. A verdict of accidental death was passed.

William Heath (57), from Old Heath in Shrewsbury, was a coal merchant by trade and had been a member of Shrewsbury Town Council. He met his death in a tragic accident at Shrewsbury railway station, but on the forecourt rather than the railway line. It was 8 January 1887 when Heath approached the forecourt, spoke briefly to a nearby shopkeeper and then went looking for a cab. The cabbies at the time would gather under the shelter of a large canopy attached to the brick wall below the Dana footpath. Heath was seen by cabman John Clews to enter the 'cabstand' apparently looking for another cabman. Clews had been standing under the canopy, but moved away to tend to his horse and when Heath moved to the spot he had just vacated, the whole stand collapsed on top of him. A witness by the name of David Reece described the sound as like 'walnuts being cracked on a wooden floor.' It transpired later that the fatal collapse was caused by a huge accumulation of snow on the roof which had thawed slightly, slipped downwards and caused the immense pressure which had torn it from the retaining wall.

When the debris was removed, Heath was found in a kneeling position with two rafters resting on his shoulders. Both his legs were broken as well

The canopy at Shrewsbury Railway Station which collapsed under the weight of snow in January 1887 with fatal consequences. In the foreground is the Clement memorial obelisk in its original position (see chapter 2)

as a number of ribs and he was declared dead by a local GP. The general consensus seems to have been that it was a miracle that more people were not killed on what was a busy market day. There could at times be up to 15 cabbies sheltering under the stand as well as passengers. It was only the fact that it was 'hailing time' and many were out touting for business that prevented an even greater tragedy.

The event propelled Shrewsbury, albeit briefly, into the national media spotlight with substantial reports appearing in *The Post*, *The Daily Gazette* and even *The Times*. An inquest was convened under the Borough Coroner **R.E. Clarke (132)**. At the outset, criticism was levelled at the railway company for disturbing the debris before it could be examined by the jury. The explanation given was that a man who had lost his young son insisted that it all be removed for fear the lad lay underneath. Nevertheless, the railway company were expressly forbidden from disturbing the debris further.

Much discussion centred on the construction of the cabstand. A local architect, Mr J.L. Randal, was called in for a professional opinion. He reported that the structure had fulfilled its purpose adequately for something like 30 years. However, the iron pillars of the stand were let into the stone-work to a depth of only 1½ inches, they were not pinned and the rafters were only 'spiked' onto the wall-plate. When the spikes gave way under the enormous weight of snow, the whole structure collapsed. Mr Randal was cautious however in his conclusions. He said that had he been erecting the stand himself he might have done it differently, but 'for the purpose intended it was properly constructed.'

The jury were less reticent: they returned a verdict of 'accidental death', but formally expressed the view that the cabstand was not properly constructed.

5 ACCIDENTAL DEATH

Farnborough airfield in Hampshire has a long and proud history going back to the earliest days of military aviation. The very first powered flight in the UK took place there in 1908 and, prior to the First World War, balloons and airships were developed at the airfield for military use. During the Great War itself the Royal Flying Corps (RFC) was based at Farnborough as was the official Army aircraft factory. Military flying only ended at Farnborough as recently as 1994.

It was there on 8 February 1922 that **Flight Lieutenant Robert C. Jenkins (162)** met his death in a flying accident, at the age of 26. Jenkins was a flying instructor, described as, 'a very excellent pilot' who had done a great deal of instructional work. Piloting the plane in which Jenkins died, under instruction from him, was Observer Officer A. Hesketh. The two were in contact by telephone and the plane was fitted with dual control. Hesketh survived the crash though he suffered head injuries. It was his second miraculous escape in the space of a year. On 24 February 1921 he was flying with Flying Officer W.L.G. Spinney when the plane crashed killing Spinney.

Hesketh was making his second training flight of the day when Ft Lt Jenkins met his death. They took off against the wind and cleared some small trees within the airfield perimeter, flew low over the A325 Farnborough Road but crashed in the nearby Deepcut Dairy when the wing caught a large tree, turning the plane completely over. It was 'smashed to splinters' and Jenkins suffered a fractured skull. He never regained consciousness and died later the same day.

The Inquest heard that the plane's engine had been checked and found to be in good working order. In addition, both Hesketh himself and a number of witnesses reported no indication of engine failure as the plane rose from the ground. The jury, however, seeking a rational explanation and relying heavily on the evidence of Observer Officer F.L. Kingham, who described the engine as 'missing' as it passed over the sick quarters, recorded a verdict of accidental death due to partial engine failure.

His death brought to an end an outstanding career in both military and civil life. Jenkins was educated at Charterhouse and Sandhurst. He served in

France in early 1915, where he was badly wounded, mentioned in despatches for 'gallant conduct' and, as a result, received the Military Cross. In 1916 he joined the RFC and served in two successful campaigns in Egypt, when he was again mentioned in despatches. After the War, Jenkins worked on a survey of the famous 'Cape to Cairo' route and was presented with the Order of the Nile by the Sultan of Egypt. In 1919–20 he served in Baghdad at a time of local uprisings and was made an MBE. He then returned to England to take up instructional duties with (what had by then become) the RAF at Farnborough.

In a letter following his death, Jenkins' commanding officer described him as, 'dead straight, absolutely legal in everything he did and said, full of infectious energy and a wonderful combination of manly pluck and determination.' His coffin was brought from Farnborough to Shrewsbury by rail, accompanied by the firing and bearer parties and a detachment of officers and men of the 4th Squadron of the RAF in which he had served. The funeral service at Shrewsbury Cemetery was taken by the Ven. G.W. Jeudwine, Archdeacon of Lincoln, after which three volleys were fired over his grave.

Ft Lt Jenkins came from a proud military family who lived at Cruckton Hall near Hanwood. Other members of his family are buried in Shrewsbury Cemetery, including his grandfather, **Major General Charles Vanbrugh Jenkins (162)**, who died on 10 December 1892 at the age of 70. His gravestone records the fact that he was the 'late Colonel commanding 19th Hussars'. Another relative, **Edgar Francis Jenkins (162)**, was one of the leading ecclesiastical solicitors of his generation until his death in 1898 aged only 47 (see Chapter Seven).

Cruckton Hall near Hanwood, once home of the Jenkins family

Freda Gossman (50), a 31-year-old spinster, and her friend **Winifred Knowles (50)**, aged 25, are buried near each other in the older Catholic section of the Cemetery, near Longden Road. They both died in a major fire which started backstage at the Paris Opera Comique House on 26 May 1887. Opera Comique had developed in France as a 'light and pleasing' antidote to standard opera, which audiences were beginning to find over-serious and boring; it included a spoken narrative involving jokes and opinions poking fun at the opera's main characters. Opera Comique was the equivalent of the German 'Singspiel', examples of which include Mozart's *Magic Flute* and Beethoven's *Fidelio*.

There was a large number of deaths in the disastrous fire and they included a group of lady friends who were staying together in Paris. Amongst these were Winifred Knowles, who had been living on the Continent for some time, but was a regular visitor to her family home in Shropshire. She was the daughter of Mr Charles Knowles, a retired Customs Officer from Hadnall. Another member of the party, her cousin, Mrs Summers, was the daughter of Charles Knowles' brother, an Alderman from Gloucester. Their friend, Miss Freda Gossman, was German.

During an evening out at the opera, they were caught up in a huge fire which consumed much of the opera house. They desperately sought refuge in the Refreshment Room, but to no avail and died there from asphyxiation; Miss Knowles' watch stopped at precisely 6.05am. Having received no response to a series of telegrams, Mr W. Summers travelled to Paris with his brother-in-law only to receive the terrible news of the death of his wife and friends.

Miss Knowles' and Miss Gossman's coffins were brought by train to Shrewsbury via Gloucester. Following a short service in the Roman Catholic cathedral on Town Walls, Miss Knowles was buried in the same grave as her mother and Miss Gossman in a separate adjacent grave. The reason for Miss Gossman's body being brought to England for burial remains something of a mystery. It seems likely that she had no close family to make funeral arrangements nearer home. A further factor may have been French burial regulations which could have resulted in her body being exhumed should regular payments not be kept up on her grave.

The history of Shrewsbury Flower Show goes back to at least 1875 when a small group of enthusiasts under the chairmanship of the then Mayor, **Joshua Pugh White (182)**, hatched plans for what was to become proudly known as The World's Wonder Show. Almost from the outset, special attractions were laid on to help bring in the crowds. Over the years, these included military bands, hot-air balloon flights, acrobats and tight rope walkers. Amongst these was a certain **Gustav Pedina (75)**, described in advertisements for the 1901 show as 'Pedina, Sensational Mast Performer, 100 feet high.' Sadly, spectators at the Show were never to enjoy his performances. Pedina had been injured when he fell off a 'swinging mast' some months before at the Crystal Palace and his performance at Shrewsbury Flower Show was to be his first since the accident. However, Pedina, according to Horticultural Society records, 'came to Shrewsbury on the Monday with the intention of carrying out his engagement, but he was taken seriously ill and gradually sank until the Wednesday night when he expired'. The thoughtfulness and care with which Shrewsbury Horticultural Society dealt with such an unexpected situation is worthy of

note. They swiftly resolved to pay all the expenses of his medical treatment and funeral (a total of £20 15s), and presented his widow with £10 to assist her to return to her home in Germany. The Cemetery record lists his occupation as 'acrobat' and he is buried in an unmarked grave near the western edge of the Cemetery's 'great grave circle'.

Fortunately for spectators, the resourceful organisers of the Show were able to make a last minute replacement booking: Pablo Diaz from Cuba, who was billed as 'the greatest contortionist in the world'.

Shrewsbury Cemetery contains at least 12 memorials to local people who lost their lives by drowning. Perhaps not entirely surprisingly, three lost their lives in the River Severn and another in the nearby River Rea. Two drowned whilst still in their childhood: **Kenneth Jeffries (17)** (died 1919) was only 14 and **Bertie France (77)** a mere 3½ when he drowned in 1911. Spare a thought also for **Thomas and Margaret Dixon**

Major Wilmsdorff G. Mansergh was killed in March 1893 at the age of 55 by 'being thrown from his car'. His tombstone in the cemetery also records that he was a 'Staff Paymaster ...[who] Served Queen and country 37 years and took part in the Egyptian Campaign on the Nile in 1882'. This was the year after the Mahdi had come to the notice of the Egyptian authorities

48

(148) who lost two of their sons by drowning, one aged 27 near Kinsale in Ireland in 1852 and a second aged 28 near Singapore in 1861.

Two of those whose memorials stand in Shrewsbury Cemetery gave their lives in heroic attempts to save others. **Henry Armstrong (105)** was a native of Shrewsbury and a coachbuilder by trade. He was on holiday at the time of his death at Clarach Bay near Aberystwyth, a favourite bathing place. It was August 1909 and Mr G.H. Cartwright, a teacher from West Bromwich, was bathing in the sea. The tide was high at the time, however, and having ventured too far from the shore he found himself out of his depth. His desperate cries for help could not be heard by those on the beach, but visitors on nearby Constitution Hill were able to shout a warning to them. Armstrong, who was dressing having just come out of the sea, immediately grabbed a rope and swam out to Cartwright intending that those on the beach should pull them both to safety. Unfortunately, the rope was of insufficient length, so he was left supporting Cartwright as best he could. He was eventually forced to release him due to sheer exhaustion, but by then two other men had swum out to try and help with the rescue. Their brave efforts were in vain, however, as both Cartwright and Henry Armstrong — unable to sustain themselves longer — disappeared below the waves.

An Inquest was held on both men a few days later. The Revd Percy Thompson from Sevenoaks, an eye-witness, gave evidence that he believed both lives would have been saved had there been any life-saving apparatus at all nearby: 'There was nothing at hand but a wretched piece of rope.' he said. The jury recorded a verdict of 'accidental drowning' and expressed sympathy with the relatives. Armstrong was 47 years old. He was buried in Aberystwyth, but his death is recorded on his family gravestone back home in Shrewsbury.

Bray in County Wicklow is one of Ireland's largest and longest-established seaside resorts. On 12 August 1955 **Sidney Jones (Plot 3)**, a railwayman from Crewe Street in Shrewsbury, was enjoying a day out there with his 16-year-old son, Derek. The two were on holiday together in Dublin and were due to return home in a few days. As they relaxed on the beach in front of Bray's splendid 19th century esplanade, they heard cries for help from Gerald Long, a resident of Bray, who had got into difficulties whilst bathing too far from the shore. A number of people went to his aid, including Derek and his father. However, both got into difficulties themselves. Whilst Derek and Gerald Long were brought safely to shore by the other rescuers, Sidney Jones sadly lost his life.

At an Inquest held the following day, the Coroner, Mr J.P. Brennan, said that Mr Jones' actions were 'worthy of the highest notice' and should be brought to the attention of the proper British authorities. He went on to say that the number of similar cases he had had to deal with that summer was far too high and due largely to the complete absence of any proper life-saving equipment at the beach. 'It does seem to me to be a matter of grave concern that in a place like Bray, frequented by so many bathers from the home territory as well as abroad, to see that no provision is made whatever for life-saving,' he concluded.

It was left to the police in Shrewsbury to inform Mr Jones' wife of the tragedy, which occurred on the eve of the 15th birthday of their daughter, Barbara.

One poignant entry in the Cemetery Register records the burial on 27 September 1921 of 'an unknown man found drowned in the Severn'. His age was said to be 'about 65' and he was buried in a 'common grave' at the southern end of the Cemetery. The Register entry states that his body was removed from the parish of Shrawardine, a village which stands a few miles west of Shrewsbury on the banks of the river.

6   THE AUTHORESS AND THE ROSE-GROWER

On the face of it, Mary Webb, the authoress, and Hilda Murrell, the rose-grower, may seem to have little in common. Mary Webb was born in 1881 and died in 1927 at the tragically young age of 46. She was already 25 when in 1906 Hilda Murrell was born. Hilda, however, lived to be 79, having experienced developments and changes which the authoress could never have even dreamed of. What links the two is that they were both native Salopians, both loved the natural world and were peace-loving and gentle people who both died tragic deaths, though in very different circumstances.

Mary Webb (15) was born at Leighton, a small village on the River Severn near Ironbridge, on 25 March 1881. On both sides of her family she had strong Celtic ancestry. George Edward Meredith, her father, was proud of his Welsh descent while her mother, Sarah Alice, was the only child of a rich Edinburgh surgeon, a member of the Scott clan. Mary was their first child and eldest by six years of the five other Meredith children.

When Mary was still a baby the family moved to Much Wenlock to a much larger house, known as The Grange, where they lived from 1882 to 1896. There her father expanded his private boarding school and also kept a 'home farm'. He was a cultured man who wrote poetry, painted and was a great lover of nature. He was adored by the young Mary, who would listen intently as he talked of the history, folklore and legends of Shropshire. She was educated

Leighton Lodge,
where Mary Webb was born

initially in her father's school, and then by a Governess, Miss Lory (known affectionately as Minoni). At 14 she was sent to a Finishing School in Southport for two years, her first time away from her beloved Shropshire. Already she was beginning to write poems, as well as stories and little plays to amuse her younger brothers and sisters. She had also developed an acute love of the natural world and a remarkable perception for its minute details. This was to inspire and colour her literary work throughout her life.

Mary Webb in her last years

The Merediths moved in 1896 to Stanton-on-Hine-Heath in north Shropshire. It was there at the age of 20 that Mary first fell ill with Graves' Disease, an incurable thyroid disorder. Resultant poor health was to dog her for the rest of her life and led ultimately to her early death. It also altered her appearance, giving her eyes a slightly bulging, staring look and resulting in a noticeable swelling, or goitre, in her neck. As a result, Mary became very self-conscious and retreated into herself. It was during a period of convalescence from her illness, however, that she wrote her first serious work of prose, *The Spring of Joy*; this was a collection of nature essays which remained unpublished until 1917, when she had already become an established novelist.

In 1902 the family moved again, this time to Meole Brace near Shrewsbury. Their new home, Maesbrook, was an old mill house with extensive wooded grounds. Mary was very happy there and slowly regained her confidence, even venturing out to attend concerts and literary events. In 1907 a terrible railway accident in Shrewsbury (see Chapter Four) prompted her to write a poem which she then quickly discarded. It was discovered, however, by her brother Kenneth and, to Mary's embarrassment, subsequently appeared in the *Shrewsbury Chronicle*. Letters received by the paper, from readers who had found solace and comfort in her words, helped to further strengthen her self-belief. A cruel blow was soon to follow though when her father died early in 1909, a loss from which Mary never fully recovered.

A year later she met a young Cambridge graduate by the name of Henry B.L. Webb (a nephew of the famous Captain Webb from Dawley — the first man to swim across the Channel). He was cultured and charming and their shared interests in literature, writing and nature helped their relationship to grow and blossom. They were engaged in 1911 and married on 12 June 1912 in Holy Trinity church, Meole Brace. Mary's unique arrangements for the wedding exasperated her mother, but delighted her new husband — the 70 guests were old and destitute people she had come to know, mostly from Cross Houses workhouse. Her only bridesmaid was 3½-year-old Winifred, daughter of the family's gardener, Tom Downes.

After the wedding, Mary and Henry travelled to Weston-super-Mare, where he was working as a teacher, to start a new life in a town she did not know and far from the Shropshire she loved and missed. It was not a happy period in her life, but in exile she began writing her first novel, *The Golden Arrow*. The book was set amongst the Stiperstones and Long Mynd hills, a part of Shropshire she knew well. In her central character, the strong gentle shepherd John Arden, she created an image and memory of her father.

With Mary unable to settle in distant Somerset, the Webbs returned to Shropshire in 1914 and rented an isolated cottage in Pontesbury. The prospect of a rural life in Shropshire with Henry at home all day was a source of deep happiness to Mary. They planned to live on an allowance she received from Scott family funds, supplemented by income from their writing. They also grew their own fruit and vegetables and kept bees for honey. Mary sold their flowers and vegetables at Shrewsbury Market, often walking there and back. It was in Pontesbury that she completed *The Golden Arrow* and wrote her second novel *Gone to Earth*. The First World War affected her deeply. Three of her brothers served on the Western Front and the dark mood of parts of *Gone to Earth* was a reaction to the horror and carnage of war. It received much critical acclaim, including a favourable review by John Buchan.

In 1917 Henry and Mary achieved a long-held ambition of buying their own home. With the sale of Mary's novels going reasonably well and Henry working as a teacher again — at the Priory School in Shrewsbury — they had a small bungalow built on Lyth Hill. Here she seems to have found a degree of peace and drew inspiration for her novels and poems. It was at Spring Cottage that she wrote *The House in Dormer Forest*, probably the lightest and most humorous of her novels. By now publishers were vying for the rights to her books. In typical fashion, Mary spent much of the earnings from the book on presents for local children. It was one of the sadnesses of her life that she and Henry never had children themselves, and one which she described achingly in her poem *The Neighbour's Children*:

They run to meet me, clinging to my dress,
The neighbour's children. With a wild unrest
And sobbings of a strange, fierce tenderness,
I snatch them to my breast.
But my baby, ah! my baby
Weepeth – weepeth
In the far loneliness of nonentity ...

Mary's health, however, began to deteriorate again; she suffered her first serious attack of Graves' Disease since before her marriage and this was accompanied by bouts of depression. In 1921 they moved to Bayswater in London where Henry took up a post at the King Alfred School, attracted by the challenge of teaching at one of the most progressive schools in the country. He also believed that a change of environment would benefit his wife's health and that her literary career would be aided by the contacts she could make in the capital.

This does seem to have been the case to some extent, but Mary nevertheless was desolate to be away from her beloved Shropshire. They had retained Spring Cottage and Mary returned there frequently to seek solace and inspiration. Tensions were beginning to appear in their relationship. Henry was revelling in his new career, but Mary yearned constantly to return to Shropshire although, when there, hated to be apart from Henry.

Mary Webb's grave

Seven for a Secret, her fourth novel, was published in 1922, and Mary was undertaking a lot of book reviews for leading journals such as *The Spectator* and *The Bookman*. Two years later she was awarded the Prix Femina Vie Heureuse, a coveted literary prize, for arguably her best novel *Precious Bane*, a story set amongst the meres of north Shropshire in the early 19th century. Her work continued to be praised by discerning critics, and Prime Minister Stanley Baldwin wrote to her to say how much he had enjoyed *Precious Bane*. Nevertheless, true popular success continued to elude her and was not to arrive until after her death.

By 1926, her health was failing as well as her marriage. Henry was forming a close friendship with one of his ex-pupils, Kathleen Wilson (whom he was later to marry); Kathleen even accompanied them on one of their trips back to Spring Cottage. She was pretty, vivacious and intelligent and Mary felt increasingly unable to compete. There were money problems also, though Mary continued to give generously to beggars in the London streets. She spent the summer of 1927 alone at Spring Cottage and in late September, though almost too ill to make the journey, travelled to St Leonard's in Sussex to be close to her former governess, Miss Lory. She died there in a nursing home on 8 October at the age of 46

Her body was returned to Shropshire for burial in Shrewsbury Cemetery on a fine October afternoon. She was buried beneath a lime tree in the higher part of the Cemetery, from where the 'hills of home' could be seen in the distance. Gathered round her grave were Henry, members of her family including her brother Kenneth, Miss Lory and several friends from Lyth Hill. Her death went almost unnoticed in the press and literary world, but six months later she was to become posthumously famous when Prime Minister Baldwin acclaimed her work in a speech at the Royal Literary Fund Dinner. Newspapers reported his tribute to 'this neglected genius' and the public clamoured to buy her books. In 1928, the *Collected Works of Mary Webb* was published by Jonathan Cape. It included her five novels as well as the unfinished *Armour wherein he Trusted*, her short stories, poems and nature essays. They were best sellers throughout the 1930s and went into many editions.

The second half of the 20th century saw a revival of interest in her work. In 1949, Michael Powell and Emeric Pressburger made a movie of *Gone to Earth*. It was filmed largely on the Stiperstones and in Much Wenlock and starring Oscar-winning actress, Jennifer Jones. More recently, *Precious Bane* has been televised and in the 1970s the Mary Webb Society was formed to perpetuate her memory and encourage interest in her work. It is members of the Society who today carefully tend her grave in the Cemetery.

The name of **Hilda Murrell (149)** is now well-known. Sadly, this owes more to the manner of her death than to her many qualities and achievements.

Hilda Murrell

On 21 March 1984 she was brutally assaulted in her home on Sutton Road, Shrewsbury, driven in her own car to an isolated lane about five miles east of the town and left in a poplar plantation on the far side of a ploughed field to die a lonely and agonising death from hypothermia.

Police enquires revealed that she had been out shopping in her car and had then returned home to change before going out to lunch. The house had been systematically searched and money taken, so clearly someone was either in the house or had followed her in. The intruder then drove the old lady to nearby Haughmond Hill, dragged or carried her across an open field and left her to die having stabbed her several times. Her obituary in *The Times* concluded: 'It is an almost intolerable irony that a life so dedicated to peaceful pursuits and to the pursuit of peace, should have been terminated by an act of mindless violence.' Hilda's ashes were scattered near a stone cairn at Maengwynned on the Shropshire/Wales border near Llanfyllin. She is commemorated, however, on her family gravestone in Shrewsbury Cemetery.

Hilda Murrell was born in Shrewsbury in 1906, the elder daughter of Owen and Lily Murrell. She won a scholarship to Shrewsbury High School, where she became Head Girl, and then studied at Newnham College, Cambridge, then almost exclusively a male preserve. She graduated with an MA in English and French Literature and modern and mediaeval languages. Her father and his brother, Edwin, ran a well-known rose nursery in the Belvidere area on the eastern outskirts of Shrewsbury, an enterprise which Hilda now joined and where she worked hard to develop her horticultural and business skills. During her time with the company Murrell's won gold awards at Chelsea and Southport Flower Shows, as well as at Shrewsbury. They did business throughout the UK and in many parts of Europe and Hilda became one of Britain's leading authorities on roses, specialising in old and miniature varieties. In 1961 the business moved to agricultural land beside the by-pass, near Sutton Farm, because of the building of the new Shirehall. By then the business was under her sole management and in 1970 she sold it to Percy Thrower and retired.

During the Second World War she had put her considerable energy and organisational ability to work in the care and resettlement of refugees. She worked indefatigably and took a personal interest in several individual cases,

Hilda Murrell's house with police van during the investigation

making life-long friends as a result. Hill walking was from an early age one of her favourite activities and before and after the Second World War she pursued an interest in mountaineering and rock-climbing. This continued until arthritis in her ankles forced her, reluctantly, to scale down her activities. It was a related love of the countryside and wildlife of the Welsh Marches which prompted her, in 1962, to become a founder member of the Shropshire Conservation Trust (now the Shropshire Wildlife Trust). She served on the organisation's council for many years and was rarely less than outspoken and forthright, though always steadfastly loyal. She often found herself impatient with the slow progress made on local conservation issues and what she believed was a timid and ultra-cautious approach by the Trust on national issues. Latterly she was to become more involved in the Shropshire branch of the Council for the Protection of Rural England. Amongst other projects, she was responsible for the establishment of its Amenities Committee, which she also chaired. She also kept meticulous and detailed 'nature diaries', with fine botanical drawings, during her travels throughout Great Britain and abroad. These were later published posthumously, edited by Charles Sinker, a former director of the Field Studies Council.

From the mid 1970s onward she became increasingly committed to the campaign against what she saw as the unacceptable dangers of nuclear power generation. She strove to brief herself fully on all aspects of what is a highly technical field and when the Department of the Environment published a white paper on Radioactive Waste Management, she was ready to challenge the experts on their own ground. Because she did her homework and was unswervingly honest, her spoken and written arguments always commanded respect, and when she unashamedly used her personal charm in debate, as well as her trained intellect, even the most hard-bitten scientific expert could quake. The fact that she was the first individual objector to have a paper accepted as evidence by the Sizewell Enquiry, indicates how seriously her views were taken.

Close friends remember her as a fierce but fundamentally gentle warrior; a committed and sometimes lonely soul, constantly on a search for truth and moral justice. The other side of Hilda Murrell, however, reveals someone who could also be charming, witty, generous and welcoming. Her clarity of thought and meticulous attention to detail, made her a formidable adversary, but her warm friendship was available to all who responded to it and close relationships, once made, could last a lifetime.

In the aftermath of her vicious murder various theories were put forward to explain the motive for the crime. One related to the fact that at the time of her death she was working on a paper to present to the Sizewell Enquiry. To do this she had been in close contact with people in CND and the wider antinuclear campaign. Some of these were convinced they were under surveillance by the security services. It was also reported that in a telephone call to friends, Hilda had said that she believed her own life to be in danger. It has to be said that hers was a very public form of protest and her details, including her address, would have been readily available as they had been lodged with various official enquiries. It is also claimed that the security services regularly use private detectives for local surveillance work and to break into houses to search for incriminating documents, a scenario which has some resonance with the circumstances of her death.

Perhaps chief among the various theories, however, was that the incident

The gravestone of Laura, John and Lucretia Marshall is perhaps the most aesthetically pleasing in the cemetery

was somehow linked to the sinking of an Argentinian ship, *The Belgrano*, during the Falklands War. Claims have been made that the *Belgrano* was torpedoed at the beginning of the War in order to scupper peace talks which were taking place in Uruguay. It is suggested that Mrs Thatcher's government wanted the War and ordered the submarine, *HMS Conqueror*, to sink the ship even though they knew its patrol had ended and it was steaming away from the 'exclusion zone' and back to port.

The link between the Belgrano incident and Hilda Murrell was through her nephew, Lt Commander Rob Green. He had been a staff officer at Northwood, the Navy Command Centre. He was known as something of a dissenting voice and left the Navy after the Falklands conflict. The security services, so the theory goes, were afraid that Green had taken copies of important documents relating to the Belgrano with him. In the belief that he had left them for safe keeping with his aunt in Shrewsbury, they ransacked her house, and then, whether by accident or design, killed her. One of the leading proponents of this theory, maverick Scottish MP Tam Dalyell, claimed it came directly from a 'reliable intelligence source'.

None of the theories could be proved and gradually Hilda Murrell's story slipped out of the headlines and the public consciousness. In 2002, however, the Police instituted a review of the 3,000 statements, 500 reports, 3,000 exhibits and 6,000 lines of enquiry associated with the case. This led to a breakthrough and in June of the following year Andrew George, a 35-year-old builder's labourer from Shrewsbury, was arrested and charged with the murder. He was convicted in May 2005; he would only have been 16 at the time of her death.

In 1994, the tenth anniversary of her death, a grove of birch trees was planted in her memory at Tanybryn near Oswestry. Ten years later, in 2004, a commemorative stone was unveiled there by her nephew, Rob Green.

7   SAINTS, SOLDIERS AND OPTHALMOLOGISTS

Just to the south of the Cemetery chapel, in a slight dip, is a discreet area seemingly packed with the graves of local Victorian luminaries; amongst them is **Edwyn Andrew (102)**. After listing his many academic achievements, his gravestone records that to his 'noble exertions is due the erection of the present Shropshire and Wales Eye, Ear and Throat Hospital of which he was for 25 years Honorary Surgeon.'

Shrewsbury's Eye, Ear and Throat Hospital (now Kingsland Bridge Mansions) was opened on 21 September 1881 by the Countess of Bradford. It was, by all accounts, quite an occasion. A procession headed by the Band

Kingsland Bridge Mansions,
once Shrewsbury's Eye, Ear and Throat Hospital

of the King's Light Infantry was met by Archdeacon Allen and the choristers of St Chad's on the steps of the building and the Countess formally opened the new hospital with a silver key presented by Mr Robinson, jeweller of The Square. The sight at the opening was obviously impressive: 'The elegant staircase was thronged with ladies from town and county, attired in dresses of divers pleasing tints and colours, and arranged tier upon tier, extending almost to the summit of the building'. After the ceremony, the company retired to the Music Hall, where the Countess opened a grand bazaar which continued for three days and raised £1,229 for Hospital funds.

Shrewsbury's new hospital was a striking example of the Victorian mock gothic style and, it is said, was later described by poet John Betjeman as the finest piece of Victorian architecture he had seen. It was designed by C.O. Ellison, who had previously designed a similar building in Liverpool. The contractors, Treasure and Sons of Shrewsbury, used pressed red bricks and terra cotta from the Trefynant works at Ruabon.

As an institution, however, the Hospital was already some 60 years old. A proposal to open a dispensary in Shrewsbury for the relief of the poor of Shropshire and Mid Wales suffering from diseases of the eye and ear, was first made in 1818. An enthusiastic member of the founding committee, Dr G.F.D. Evans (known, because of his initials, as 'Alphabet' Evans) offered a room in his house in Castle Street for the use of the Dispensary, and for the next thirteen years appears to have been the only doctor working there. The room measured a mere 7 by 17 feet and the Dispensary was open for two hours on Wednesday and Saturday mornings. Around 150 patients were treated there each year.

It was financed by annual subscriptions of a guinea and by benefactions of upwards of five guineas. Both subscribers and benefactors were entitled to recommend two patients annually for treatment. Funds were made available to help patients from a distance pay for lodgings in the town. In its early years, however, most of the patients came from Shrewsbury or nearby, the majority suffering from cataracts, accidental injuries or infant blindness. This last affliction was usually caused by bathing inflamed eyes in milk, a popular remedy at the time, but one which induced tubercular infections and subsequent blindness.

In 1832 Dr Evans retired, to be replaced by Dr Edwin Foulkes who threw great energy into his new role and the work of the Dispensary. Foulkes was a well-known character in the town and was described later by local cleric, Prebendary Auden, as 'a man of social habits, fond of company, and not unaccustomed to take part in practical jokes which in his time were a fashionable amusement inherited from the Regency.' During the 30 years of Foulkes' appointment the number of patients increased, and by 1836 the total number of patients treated at the Dispensary since its foundation was 3,583. Subscriptions, however, did not keep pace and when he died in 1861 it was feared the Dispensary might have to close.

Fortunately for the Hospital, his successor was Dr Edwyn Andrew, a Cornishman of great commitment, under whose leadership it entered a new and vital phase. It was a time of great advances and innovations in medicine and Andrew introduced some of them to his hospital; they included the use of chloroform. He also obtained permission from the committee to purchase a box of test spectacles for the use of his patients, something his predecessors had apparently not felt the need for.

Andrew also called for a brand new hospital to be built, but ultimately had to settle for the old Penitentiary (a home for reformed prostitutes) at 8 Dogpole. The building was purchased for £400; it was not ideal, but did provide five beds for in-patients, a waiting room, operating theatre and consulting room. Dr Andrew made frequent visits to different London eye hospitals and tried to model his new Dispensary on what he had seen there. The new premises were opened in late 1866 and Mr Soelburg Wells, Professor of Opthalmology at Kings College, was appointed consultant surgeon. In Andrew's first year at Dogpole 358 patients were treated, 45 of them as in-patients. They came from as far afield as Wolverhampton, Radnor and Towyn and large industrial firms, among them the Coalbrookdale and Madeley Wood companies, were taking out subscriptions.

By 1872 Dr Andrew was already contemplating a move to larger premises and it was decided to launch an appeal. With indefatigable energy, Andrew also set about raising still more subscriptions from companies in Shropshire and Wales. Between 1867 and 1877, the number of patients and subscriptions doubled. In 1875, the word throat was added to the name of the Hospital, although it was stressed at the time that only infections of the throat which caused injury to the ears could be treated.

No. 8 Dogpole, the location of the new hospital opened in 1866

By 1879 a plot of land in Murivance, an area described at the time as 'the Madeira of Shrewsbury', due to its sheltered position overlooking the Severn, was purchased for £2,000. Soon afterwards the foundation stone of a new building was laid by the Earl of Powis. The architect C.O. Ellison won the competition to design the new hospital but the selection of his design was not without controversy as there was much elaborate ornamentation, the cost of which met some criticism. It is recorded that one committee member stated: 'When the new building collapses, it could be turned into a hotel to be known as Andrew's Folly.'

Nevertheless the building work continued and Shrewsbury's new Eye, Ear and Throat Hospital was formally opened on 21 September 1881. Although the exterior was mock Gothic, the concept and interior design were forward looking and innovative. The emphasis throughout was on open space, light and air, a far cry from many hospitals in the 19th century. The modern features included central heating, gas for cooking, telephones, electric bells, speaking tubes and lifts to take food to patients. Patients generally were delighted with their accommodation and treatment, but one old lady, who had been allowed beer when treated at Dogpole, was heard to comment: 'The new hospital may be very beautiful, no doubt, but there's too much air and too little beer, so I prefer the old place.'

Less than six years after the opening of the new edifice in Murivance, Dr Edwyn Andrew died, aged only 55, and was buried in Shrewsbury Cemetery. The Hospital, which owed so much to his commitment, imagination and hard work, continued to go from strength to strength. During the First World War, up to 800 servicemen with eye injuries

The grave of E.H. Van Tromp 'erected ... as a memento of the respect and esteem in which he was held for his public services and private worth ... ever foremost in promoting the best interests of the Borough of S'bury and by his geniality and courtesy, by his force of character and enthusiasm ... etc etc!'

were treated every week. The original hospital had about 25 beds on two floors of wards, but in 1926 an extension created more wards and improved out-patient facilities, almost doubling its size. The Hospital became part of the new NHS in 1948 and 'Andrew's Folly' only finally closed its doors in 1998, after 116 years of service.

The services provided by the Eye, Ear and Throat Hospital in Murivance have been transferred to the Royal Shrewsbury Hospital and with them a set of beautiful portraits of Faith, Hope and Charity which can be seen in the reception area there. The building was purchased by Shropshire Homes who renovated and converted it into smart, modern apartments known rather grandly as Kingsland Bridge Mansions.

At the outset of the Second World War, a gentleman by the name of **Martin Zade (102)** came to Shrewsbury to work at the Eye, Ear and Throat Hospital. He had previously been Professor of Opthalmology at Heidelberg University. Zade spent three years in Shrewsbury assisting a Dr Anderson, but was to die on 3 April 1944, aged 66. He was buried in the Cemetery very close to Dr Andrew's grave. His memorial stone bears a quotation from Goethe which translates roughly as:

> That you have no ending
> Makes you great
> And that you have no beginning
> That is your fate.

Someone with a very different background and life-story was **Corporal Henry Preece (166)**. His gravestone proudly proclaims that he 'served in the Crimean War, taking part in the charge of the heavy brigade at Balaclava.' The Charge of the Heavy Brigade was one of the British Army's most brilliant military achievements, but has been almost entirely overshadowed by the glorious failure of the Charge of the Light Brigade. In the engagement in which Henry Preece played his part, 600 men led by General James Yorke Scarlett routed around 2,000 of the Russian cavalry. British and French forces had begun the siege of Sebastopol on 17 October 1854 and the attack on the British-held port of Balaclava was an attempt by Russian forces to relieve the siege. There were three main actions in the battle of Balaclava: the unsuccessful Russian cavalry charge against the 'thin red line' of British Highlanders, the successful charge of the British Heavy Brigade and the debacle involving the British Light Brigade. The Heavy Brigade was a grouping of cavalry units consisting of six squadrons from the Royal Scots Greys, the Inniskillin Dragoons and the Dragoon Guards. The job of the Heavy Brigade was to smash through enemy lines and that is what they achieved.

North of Balaclava harbour is a ridge of hills known as the Causeway Heights which were defended by Turkish soldiers in six redoubts. On the morning of 25 October a huge Russian force attacked the Turks. Initially the attack was successful, the Russians captured some redoubts and pressed on. However, they were held up by the 93rd Highlanders under the command of Sir Colin Campbell. William Howard Russell, the *Times* correspondent, described them as 'a thin red streak tipped with a line of steel' — later shortened in popular parlance to 'the thin red line'. The Highlanders drove off the Russian cavalry on their front, but 2,000 or so Russians came down the hill towards the British headquarters and the Heavy Brigade with its 600 men.

In command of this Brigade was General Scarlett, whose first ever battle this was going to be. The Russians had caught him unprepared and at a disadvantage on lower ground. But, in spite of this, he decided to charge uphill. Scarlett's troop officers started to form up unhurriedly, almost as if on the parade ground. Without apparent concern, they turned their backs on the enemy until they were ready. The incredulous Russians halted in their tracks and for a moment silence reigned. The distance between the two cavalries at last decreased to around 50 yards and the shrill sound of a trumpet ordering the charge broke the silence.

When the charge sounded Scarlett calmly led his troops forward into the heart of the enemy. For some time it looked as though the Heavy Brigade had been completely enveloped and was about to be destroyed. Luckily, at that moment reinforcements arrived in the shape of the 4th Dragoon Guards. There was terrible confusion, but despite being hampered by blunt and rusty swords caused by the wet weather, in only eight minutes the Russians had been put to 'utter rout'.

Henry Preece, according to his obituary in the *Shrewsbury Chronicle* (and no doubt the stories he told in later years) played a prominent part in the charge and 'many of the enemy died by his hand'. At one point he was attacked by two Russian horsemen and, despite a severe wound which nearly severed his nose, pursued the retreating Russians for a considerable distance, having great difficulty then in finding his way back to his regiment. At the end of the battle he was complimented by the Colonel of the 4th Dragoon Guards and later awarded the Distinguished Conduct Medal (DCM). The Charge of the Heavy Brigade, in which Henry Preece made his name, was later immortalised in a poem by Alfred Lord Tennyson. It begins:

> The charge of the gallant three hundred, the Heavy Brigade!
> Down the hill, down the hill, thousands of Russians,
> Thousands of horsemen, drew to the valley – and stay'd;
> For Scarlett and Scarlett's three hundred were riding by
> When the points of the Russian lances arose in the sky ...

Preece recovered from his wounds and continued his military service, being present at the fall of Sebastopol when he was Orderly to Brigadier General Sir Edward Cooper Hodge. As the city fell, Hodge said to his Orderly: 'Remember Preece that you are the first British Dragoon to enter Sebastopol.'

Much later, in the summer of 1891, when Henry Preece was 61, his old regiment marched through Shrewsbury en route from Ireland to Aldershot. By arrangement, he met them outside the town 'mounted on a splendid white charger' and rode proudly at their head into The Square. In retirement, he became landlord of the London Apprentice on Coton Hill where for many years he hosted an annual Balaclava Dinner. Those who attended 'remember vividly the stories of doughty deeds in days gone by with which they were always entertained by their host.'

He died aged 77 in June 1907 and was buried in Shrewsbury Cemetery. He was accompanied to his last resting place by a 'body of aged veterans' who had fought in the Crimea with him, the Indian Mutiny, New Zealand, Ashanti and the Abyssinian, Zulu and other wars. His coffin was draped with a Union Jack and placed on top were the sword and helmet he wore in the Charge of the Heavy Brigade.

Someone who also played his part in the famous charge was **Trumpet-Major Thomas Monks (26)**. Monks was born at Lancaster in 1830 and enlisted in the Inniskillin Dragoons at the age of 13, serving as a trumpeter. In 1854 he went with his regiment to Crimea as part of General Yorke Scarlett's Heavy Brigade. He was the General's trumpeter at the Charge, staying alongside his leader and coming out without a wound. He was also commended for his care of his 'charger' — he kept the same horse throughout the Crimean campaign, unlike many of his comrades who had horses shot from under them or lost them to disease or winter conditions. Monks was awarded the French Military Medal for his service in the Crimea, one of only three awarded to members of his regiment. On return to England in 1856 the regiment was reviewed at Aldershot by Queen Victoria. Monks and another NCO (Non-commissioned Officer) were chosen to approach the royal carriage and to pass on the Queen's complimentary remarks to their comrades.

Monks retired from regular service in 1872, with the Long Service and Good Conduct medal, and settled in Shrewsbury where he joined the staff band of the Shropshire Militia. In 1875 he also joined the band of the Shropshire Yeomanry and was later appointed their Trumpet-Major. In 1900 he offered to resign but the regiment's Colonel declined and Monks was kept on the Yeomanry's strength for life at the Colonel's expense, in recognition of his service. He died of pneumonia on 25 May 1902 aged 72. His funeral cortege went from his home in Port Hill Road to the Cemetery, being escorted by a detachment of the Shropshire Yeomanry led by Lord Berwick, the Staff

Sergeants of the King's Shropshire Light Infantry and a carriage-load of local military and naval veterans.

Edgar Francis Jenkins (162) came from a largely military family living at the time at Cruckton Hall near Hanwood, but Edgar chose a career in the law, ultimately rising to the very heights of his profession. During his lifetime he was no stranger to tragedy and his first wife, Marianne Brooks, died the year after their marriage, in 1884. He married again, however, in 1887 to Edith Turner by whom he had a son and daughter. Edgar himself was to die at the young age of 47 in January 1898. By then he had made his home in London, though the family were living at Cruckton Hall which they had inherited in 1879 from the Harries family. In 1875, Francis Harries, also Lord of Broseley manor, died without issue having made his cousin, **Major General Charles Vanbrugh Jenkins (162)** (Edgar's father) his heir. When Francis Harries' brother, Lt Col Thomas Harries, died four years later, the Hall passed to the Jenkins family.

A memorial service was held for Edgar Jenkins at All Saints church, Norfolk Square in the capital. He had expressed the wish, however, to be buried back in Shropshire and his body was brought by rail, in a glass funeral car, to be buried near to numerous other members of his family in Shrewsbury Cemetery.

Jenkins had risen to become the leading ecclesiastical solicitor of his generation, involved in all the major ritual and ecclesiastical cases of the 25 years before his death. He was head of the firm of Brooks, Jenkins & Co, proctors and notaries, London, a member of the Corporation of London and one of His Majesty's Lieutenants for the City of London. His final case was the celebrated one of *Read and others v the Bishop of Lincoln*, in which he successfully defended the Bishop.

In this case, Edward King, the Bishop of Lincoln, was tried before the Archbishop of Canterbury and six other Bishops on charges levelled against him by the Church Association. The Association had been formed in 1865 by several leading evangelical churchmen to maintain what they saw as the Protestant ideals of faith and worship in the Church of England. King stood accused of consecrating the bread and wine of communion whilst looking eastward rather than at the congregation, having lighted candles on the altar, mixing water and wine in the chalice and absolving and blessing with the sign of the cross. Many of these, it has to be said, were later to become common practice in the Church.

Edward King was educated at his home in Kent by his father's curate, John Day. The two became close and King followed him when he moved first to Flintshire and then to be vicar of Ellesmere. King seems to have become a sort of lay assistant to the vicar, organising amongst other things, Men's

Bible Classes and the church choir. At the age of 18 he went to Oriel College, Oxford and was later, in 1858, to become Chaplain of Cuddesdon Theological Seminary near Oxford. He served as Principal of the Seminary from 1863 to 1873, as well as being vicar of Cuddesdon. After 15 years at the Seminary, he returned to University life as Regus Professor of Pastoral Theology at Christ Church, Oxford. It was there that he first gained something of a reputation as a High Churchman, though he was far from rigid and opinionated in his beliefs.

In 1885, amidst some controversy, Archbishop Edward Benson put King's name forward for the Bishoprics of London, Exeter and Lincoln. Ironically it was Benson who was later to try him in the celebrated Read case. Prime Minister Gladstone was determined, in the face of much opposition from the Church Association and others, to have both high and low churchmanship recognised in the leadership of the Church. Although Benson expressed the view that King's powers would be 'lost on the Lincolnshire Wolds', he was offered and accepted the position of Bishop of Lincoln.

Throughout his career, King had never masked his high churchmanship; he wore vestments at a time when that was still a comparatively rare practice. He also became well-known for wearing a mitre of striking size and beauty, described at one time by a Lincolnshire farm labourer as looking exactly like a beehive. There had been something of a Catholic revival in the Church of England during Victoria's reign, beginning with the Tractarians and the Oxford Movement. Initially their concern lay with deepening theological thinking in terms of discipline, holiness and spirituality. Later, however, the Movement became centred more on ritual practice and observances. Members of the Movement, nevertheless, did not lose sight of their social responsibilities and the leading London ritualists were also the great 'slum priests', men with a passionate social concern for the poor and oppressed. Edward King shared their beliefs and commitment.

Statue of Bishop King
at Lincoln Cathedral

Conflict with the evangelical wing of the Church was inevitable and it was provoked to a large extent by a group of extremists who formed themselves into the Church Association. In the summer of 1888 they petitioned Archbishop Benson to try Edward King because of certain ritual acts which they alleged were contrary to the stipulations of the Prayer Book. These, they claimed, he had carried out in the previous December at his cathedral and the little church of St Peter-at-the-Gowts in Lincoln. The particular ritual acts for which he was tried were in fact being carried out in many parish churches at the time, but did not include what were then the main issues of controversy — the use of incense, Eucharistic vestments and statues in church.

King's trial took place in the Library at Lambeth Palace. Thanks to a large extent to the skill and knowledge of his advocate, Edgar Jenkins, his stance was upheld, though advice was proffered that he should adjust some at least of his practices. It was a notable decision in that it ignored previous important judgements made by the secular courts and the Judicial Committee of the Privy Council.

Bishop King lived and worked for a further 18 years, but never truly recovered from the strain of his trial. A close friend said that it had 'hung over him like a nightmare' and King himself, in a letter, wrote: 'I am thankful that the strain of the last three years has been removed, as it was becoming almost too much for my strength.'

Although his flock in the Lincoln diocese continued to think of him as a holy and delightful old man, the intellectual force of his public utterances had ebbed away. Bishop King died in 1910. Unlike the Roman Catholic, the Anglican Church, possessed no formal process of canonisation. Nevertheless, on 24 May 1935 it came as close to canonising Edward King as it had done anyone since the Reformation. Today, the Prayer Book still marks 8 March (the anniversary of his death) as a 'lesser festival' to commemorate the life and work of 'Edward King, Bishop of Lincoln, Teacher, Pastor.' The Collect for the day begins: 'O Almighty God, who gavest such grace unto thy servant Edward King, that whomsoever he met he drew nearer unto thee'.

King's advocate, Edgar Francis Jenkins, was to die less than eight years after the end of the trial. At his request, his body was returned to Shropshire and interred in Shrewsbury Cemetery.

There are a number of gravestones in the Cemetery which commemorate and acknowledge the lives of men who served in the local constabulary. **Sam Farlow (107)** was a native of Shrewsbury, born in the final year of the 18th century. He served in the Borough police force for nearly 40 years, rising to the rank of Superintendent in 1840 when he became 'Chief Officer of Police'. His career was closely intertwined with the life of the local Corporation and his responsibilities within the Borough of Shrewsbury were many and varied.

His gravestone is inscribed with a fulsome appreciation of his contribution:

> Here lies Sam Farlow. A name familiar and respected throughout this borough of the Police Force of which he was a member as well as a faithful servant of the Corporation for nearly forty years. He was elected Mace Bearer in 1825 and held that office until the incoming of the new Corporation in 1835. He was again appointed Superintendent of Police, Marshal, and Crier of the Court, to the Corporation in 1839, holding these offices until his death, April 7th 1857 aged 58 years ... A few of his fellow townsmen, including the Mayors under whom he served, have caused this stone to be placed over his remains, to record his long service in this Borough. September 19th 1866.

Hiram Howells (77) was born in Oswestry in 1827 of relatively humble origins. He began his working life as a labourer but, in something of a 'rags to riches' story, joined the Police at the age of 28 and rose through the ranks to become Superintendent by 1875. As his career developed, and as he bettered himself accordingly, Hiram and his family moved from one part of the county to another. The 1881 census records his eight children as having been born variously at Wellington, Cleobury Mortimer, Market Drayton and Shrewsbury. He retired after nearly 30 years' service to policing in his native county and died in November 1888 aged 61.

James Lear (60) was not a Salopian by birth, he and his wife hailed from Birmingham and he served in the Wolverhampton police force before joining the Shropshire constabulary in 1857 at the age of 26. Like Howells, he moved from station to station throughout the county as his career developed. He is known to have lived at Market Drayton, Craven Arms, Bromfield and Meole Brace and his name appears in the Quarter Session reports as having also been involved in incidents at Cressage, Dorrington and Bishop's Castle.

James Lear came to public attention, however, in 1871. On 22 October of that year, whilst serving at Bromfield, he received a report of an 'aggravated felony'. After making house to house enquiries, he came to the conclusion that a local man, Thomas Jones, was responsible. Further enquiries led him to ultimately apprehend Jones at Whettleton Common near Stokesay on 27 October. It was later estimated that he had walked upwards of 100 miles during the investigation and chase, 'during the greater part of which it had rained heavily.' As a result of his commitment and perseverance he was awarded £3 from police funds.

Lear died on 23 April 1881, he was only 50 years old and was serving as Sergeant at Meole Brace at the time of his death.

In January 1866 Colonel Edward Cureton resigned from the post of Chief Constable of Shropshire after only 15 months in the job. In the event of such a vacancy, it was usual for the county magistrates to advertise for candidates. Cureton's appointment however had been made so recently that they decided on this occasion to see if their second choice from 1864 was still available. Not only was **Colonel Richard John Edgell (191)** still available, but he had spent the intervening period in Essex studying the operation and management of the county constabulary there. Armed with a glowing reference from the Chief Constable of Essex, Edgell declared himself ready and willing to return to Shropshire and on 12 April 1866 was duly appointed as the county's fourth Chief Constable.

Edgell was quick to recognise that the force under his command was a small and relatively weak one and had been ill-equipped to deal with a number of recent incidents when armed attacks were made on the police. His efforts to change this situation bore some fruit initially and in December 1867 the Home Secretary authorised the recruitment of six extra constables making a total force of 122. In addition, when Edgell pointed out that he had only 54 cutlasses to share between his men in the event of an emergency, permission was granted for the purchase of a further 36.

It was against this background that Shrophire's police force, and its Chief Constable, faced a number of sizeable political riots late in 1867. The worst took place in Wellington where a fight broke out between mobs of Conservative and Liberal partisans. Attempts by the local police to break up the fight were immediately met with a hail of stones. After an hour of largely ineffective preventative measures, a telegram was sent to Police Headquarters in Shrewsbury. Unfortunately it arrived at the same time as one from Whitchurch requesting reinforcements to deal with similar political riots there. Orders were sent to Market Drayton and Oswestry to reinforce the police at Whitchurch but Edgell was at a loss to know what to do about Wellington as there were no spare men available. Finally he caught a train and went himself. He found 17 constables trying to control a mob of over 200 people. By 5pm it was getting dark and, with two men seriously injured, Edgell withdrew his force to the safety of the police station. Not long after that the mob dispersed and peace reigned once more in Wellington. Edgell recorded that his constables had behaved well and 'with much good temper and steadiness under great provocation'.

1867 had also been the year of the great 'Fenian' scare. This brotherhood had been formed in 1858 by Irish factions in the United States with the purpose of promoting revolution and overthrowing the English government in Ireland. In February 1867 rumours were abroad of a plot to attack Chester castle and its armoury; in September of that year a policeman was killed by the Fenians in Manchester, and in December an attempt was made to rescue prisoners from Clerkenwell prison in London. In Shropshire a report was circulating that one of the leaders of the Fenian brotherhood had visited Wellington in order to swear-in 300 Irishmen from the locality into the brotherhood. In actual fact there was nothing like that number of able-bodied Irishmen in Wellington. Nevertheless, the level of fear and panic locally and nationally was reaching a crescendo. Against this backdrop, vast numbers of special constables were recruited throughout the country. Over 1,000 were sworn-in in Shrewsbury alone. Cutlasses were also issued for use by the Shrewsbury Borough force who practiced their use in the Quarry, apparently to the consternation and alarm of some residents. Perhaps the recruitment of these special constables (over 113,000 nationally) proved sufficient for by April 1868 the Fenian brotherhood had lost heart for the fight and the panic was over.

All this must have been a disturbing experience for Colonel Edgell. He found his small and ill-equipped force facing violent and hostile mobs time and again with little means of retaliating or defending themselves. His 23 years service with Her Majesty's Bengal Army no doubt stood him in good stead but the frustrations were many. Not least amongst these was a constant tension between the county magistrates (who had overall responsibility for ordering and directing the police force) on the one hand and Edgell and the Government Inspector on the other. Many of the Inspector's ideas for strengthening and improving the efficiency of the force were rejected year after year by the magistrates. The Shropshire force was one of the weakest in the Midlands, nevertheless many of the magistrates were repeatedly hostile to the idea of recruiting extra men or increasing their pay to match that of neighbouring forces. The progress of reform and modernisation was a painfully slow one and the Shropshire force was constantly under-manned throughout the 1860s and '70s.

The appearance of police constables in Shropshire, however, was undergoing rapid change (bewilderingly so at times). Between 1868 and 1870 they, somewhat reluctantly it has to be said, put away the tall top hats which had distinguished their calling for nearly half a century and donned cloth-covered helmets. A further change in headgear occurred in 1886 when caps were supplied instead of helmets. A year later however helmets were back in vogue. The next radical change in appearance was to arrive later that same year. After 40 years of wearing distinctive rifle-green uniforms, it was decided to change the colour to blue in line with other forces. The old-style frock coats also became a thing of the past, tunics being the modern style. The only familiar remnant of the old uniform was the Oxford-grey overcoat.

Two innovations which were later to become indispensable weapons in the battle against crime were introduced during Colonel Edgell's tenure as Chief Constable. In 1870, following a successful experiment in Bristol gaol, the Home Office required that all county and borough police forces furnish the Commissioner of the Metropolitan Police with photographic likenesses of all 'habitual criminals' and in March 1889 Shrewsbury police station in Swan Hill had its first telephone installed.

The year 1889, however, was to end on a sad note for the county constabulary when on 26 November Colonel Richard Edgell, its Chief Constable, died of a heart attack. He had held office for 23 years and was hailed as an able and zealous officer who had discharged his public duties faithfully and with military exactitude.

8   ENTREPRENEURS FROM EUROPE

The **Della Porta (65)** family grave stands at the top end of Shrewsbury Cemetery, near to the boundary with Longden Road. The name of Della Porta was a familiar one in and around Shrewsbury for over 100 years. The department store owned by the family and bearing the family name stood in High Street near to The Square. It was known by generations of Salopian shoppers, not only for the vast range of goods it stocked (Della Porta's advertised itself as a 'complete home furnisher and universal provider' in the early years of the 20th century) but also for the polite and helpful service which was its hallmark.

Joseph Della Porta, a native of Moltrasio, a village on the western shore of Lake Como in Italy, came to England around 1848. He first joined the Italian community in Birmingham, working for his uncle in a wholesale

The Della Porta family grave

hardware business, and it was there he met and married an Italian girl, Rosa Peverelli. In 1857, they moved to Shrewsbury and opened a small shop in Princess Street from where Joseph operated as a 'general dealer'. It was a modest beginning and the newspapers of the time seem to have carried no advertisement urging Salopians to patronise the store. Nevertheless, as the *Shrewsbury Chronicle* reported in its obituary, 'by the exercise of energy, foresight and enterprise, he throve apace.' Slowly, Joseph built up and extended his stock, formed connections in the trade and laid a sound foundation for the future of the family business.

He was clearly an energetic and astute businessman with a singleness of purpose which he applied to the growth of his enterprise. Within a few years, he was looking for a chance to expand and then came a unique opportunity to acquire a range of buildings adjoining his shop and extending to the corner of The Square. The premises consisted of a fine Tudor building known as Lloyd's Mansion built in 1570 by David Lloyd, a prominent Shrewsbury draper. It was one of the best examples of timber frame construction in the town, with some fine original carving and moulding on the gable ends. Joseph carefully preserved the historical features of the building.

With his premises suitably extended, he was able to add new departments to the store. Ironmongery, hardware, boots and shoes were for sale as well as sewing machines and bicycles. The footwear was made on the premises, with the firm's own brand known as the 'Deltada'. Joseph, Rosa and their seven children were at this time living in quarters 'over the shop' in Princess Street and there were apprentices who also 'lived in' with the family.

As the business prospered, the Della Porta family moved to a house in Belmont. Joseph was described by contemporaries as a man of strong personality, somewhat brusque but warm-hearted. His early years in Shrewsbury were devoted to building up the firm and its reputation, it was only later that he found time for relaxation and outside interests. Although he never sought public office, the welfare of his adopted town was always close to his heart. He was involved extensively in bringing electric light to Shrewsbury and was also on the board of the Kingsland Bridge Co.

A trade review of Shropshire published in 1869 described Della Porta's as follows: 'all classes of the community flock to the establishment, for certainly nowhere in the County, and hardly out of it, can be seen such a vast and multitudinous array of goods; while in regard to prices, advantages are offered that would be extremely difficult to duplicate.' At this time, the firm was known as J. Della Porta, Son and Rabnett — the founder's son, Joseph Lewis Della Porta, and Alfred Rabnett (who had married his eldest daughter) having been taken into partnership. Rabnett later broke away and opened his own shop on the corner of Market Street and Swan Hill and the firm became simply J. Della Porta and Son.

In 1900 the principal departments were footwear, clothing, china, jewellery, fancy goods, haberdashery, stationery, furniture, ironmongery and hardware. The firm had never relied on sensational advertising or high pressure sales methods; recommendation and a high reputation were enough. It especially prided itself on its annual display of Christmas toys, gifts and cards. Della Porta's Christmas Bazaar was a veritable children's 'El Dorado', advertised locally under slogans such as 'The House of Christmas Plenty' or 'The Treasure Land of Toys'. The Victorian era, then drawing to its close, was the heyday of the toy doll, and Della Porta's boasted dolls of every nationality and of every type from princess to milk-maid.

In the early years of the 20th century, the firm was occupying numbers 1 to 3 Princess Street and 15 and 16 The Square, and had become a sizeable department store. It was approaching its half century, when the founder, Joseph Della Porta, died on 4 June 1904, aged 70. He had been ill for only a few days and had represented the Shrewsbury Bowling Club in a match at Newtown the previous week. Although by then he had handed over much of the day to day running of the store to his son, Joseph Lewis, he retained an active interest to the end.

In a report of his death, the *Shrewsbury Chronicle* praised his 'kindness and urbanity of manner' and commented that the respect he had earned as an employer was evidenced by the fact that 'there are some half dozen men who have been in his employ over 30 years, whilst others can boast over 20 years and upwards.' The funeral service was conducted by Bishop Moriarty at the Catholic Cathedral on Town Walls. As a mark of respect, business due for hearing at the Borough Police Court was adjourned and the bowling greens of the Shrewsbury and Severnside clubs closed for the day.

His son Joseph Lewis then took over full responsibility for management of the firm. Four daughters also survived him and their mother, Rosa, died on 29 December 1918; she was buried besdie her husband in Shrewsbury Cemetery.

The 1920s saw the development throughout the country of a new breed of modern department store. Della Porta's was not left behind and developed along similar lines whilst still retaining its status as a local family firm and its reputation for personal service. Business was still growing and there was a need for further expansion. Fortunately, an opportunity for this soon arose. Salop County Council had long been casting covetous eyes upon Lloyd's Mansion whch it needed for an extension to the old Shirehall which stood in The Square. At the same time, premises fronting on High Street at the rear of the existing shop became available to Della Porta's. Agreement with the County Council for the surrender of Lloyd's Mansion followed, allowing for an extensive re-building programme which extended the store into a unified whole from Princess Street through to High Street. During this expansion, Joseph Lewis Della Porta, son of the founder, died on 7 July 1929 leaving his son, Joseph William, to continue the business. He was the last family member to take an active role in it. Today, the site of the Della Porta emporium is occupied by another department store — Rackham's.

The Della Portas were not the only Italian family to move to Shrewsbury and set up a successful business. Many local people (including the author) have happy memories of being taken to a Sidoli's café in the town, a true 'cake and ice cream heaven'. The story of how Sidoli's came to be established

Lloyd's Mansion

in Shrewsbury is a real 'rags to riches' one. It begins in a remote mountain region of Italy, spans more than a century of the town's history and ends in what is today a thriving nationwide business.

The Sidoli family hails from the village of Bardi in the Ceno valley of the Appenine mountains of northern Italy. Legend has it that some time in the mid 19th century a Sidoli ancestor and other villagers crossed the mountains on foot to seek a living in the great houses of France and England. Later, in 1896, a young Tranquillo Sidoli left his home village to join a favourite sister, Scholastica, who was married to a café owner in Shrewsbury by the name of Pini. By 1908, Tranquilla had taken over 'Peeny's', as it became known, in Princess Street — just along the road from Della Porta's store. It was then that the name Sidoli first appeared above a shop in the town and with his wife, Clementina, he set about building up the business. Their son, **Dominic Sidoli (Plot 13),** was later to say, 'My parents were remarkable. They were penniless when they married and had 12 children. Life was hard but they were absolutely determined to carve out a future for their family and they did it.'

Helping them, as they developed a catering business specialising in ice creams, was a team of Italians who would spend nine months of each year in Shrewsbury and return home to their families for three months. In the early days the business of making ice cream was a painstaking labour of love. Dominic recalled: 'It started at 4am when ice cream was made by hand in big metal vats, then it had to be packed with ice. When it was ready, it was loaded into horse-drawn carts and delivered around the county. When the men returned in the evening, they had to clean the horses and carts. It was a very, very long day.'

The work paid off, as local people developed a taste for Sidoli catering, and in 1913 Tranquilla and his team were first invited to cater for Shrewsbury Flower Show. In the years that followed, Tranquilla developed his Shrewsbury

Sidoli's Café at the Music Hall

café and set up shops in Wellington and Oakengates. In 1921 he is said to have imported the very first expresso coffee machine to England. If so, his enterprise was to herald the post-war growth of coffee shops throughout the country, the birth of skiffle and the 'beat generation' and indirectly to the pop music explosion of the 1960s.

The young members of the Sidoli family were also expected to do their share of the work. After an interval at college in Italy, Dominic Sidoli joined the family business at the bottom in 1930. A few years later, when he took it upon himself to buy the latest (very costly) ice cream soda fountain for the café, which by then had moved to The Square next to the Music Hall, he was effectively sacked. He remembered later: 'It was very new, the latest shiny stainless steel model, and it made all kinds of fancy ice creams and sundaes. However, it cost £500, the price of a new house in those days. I was banished to the Oakengates shop to sell tobaccos and sweets!' Nevertheless, Dominic was re-instated five days later when his father realised he could not work the new machine, and it quickly became a crowd puller.

Dominic's brother, **Camillo Sidoli (Plot 13)**, first became really involved with the business in 1935. He was qualified as an accountant but learnt the art of ice cream making because his father wanted a specialist. He trained with Giuseppe Tanara in Parma, Italy and came back to England with a book of secret recipes which he only showed to his family in recent years. His slogan for the rich Sidoli ice cream was 'It's more than a treat, it's a food'. Before the Second World War, Tranquilla retired to Italy because of ill-health. He lived there with his wife and daughters until his death in 1976 aged 91.

An early Sidoli's ice cream vans

The War put many businesses on hold, including Sidoli's. However, there were always 'ways and means' of keeping going and, on Camillo's death in January 1999, his son, Father Paul Sidoli, recalled that Camillo had been taken to court for breaking a strict embargo on fresh cream. 'He had an arrangement with a former friend, Mr Kynaston in Minsterley and they both ended up in court. He had to pay a huge fine but it was in all the papers and he said it was the best advertisement he ever had.'

After hostilities ended, the Sidoli brothers — Dominic, Camillo, John, Renato and Aldino — set about re-building the family firm. New premises in Bellstone were opened in 1948 and refitted as an ice cream factory, bakery kitchen and restaurant. This expansion was backed up by a new convoy of ice cream vans and a further restaurant in Castle Street followed soon after. Before long, branches were opened in Chester and Wrexham in addition to those already in Wellington and Oakengates. In 1961, Sidoli's ice creams won a national award for their quality. As demand for Sidoli products grew, so the need for a larger and more up to date ice cream factory arose and in 1980 one opened in Welshpool. In 1988 the largest Sidoli restaurant of all was launched in the Telford Town Centre shopping complex.

Today, Sidoli's is still a family run firm and one of the largest gateaux and ice cream manufacturers in the country. Products from the Welshpool factory are distributed to all the major restaurant groups as well as to countries in Europe and even as far as Australia.

The story of **Hans Lobbenberg (Plot 12)** is a good example of how the dreadful events in Nazi Germany during the 1930s and 1940s came ultimately to enrich the lives, and often the economic prosperity, of the communities in which Jewish and other refugees came to settle.

Hans was born in 1896 to Jewish parents in Cologne, where his father Max ran a corsetry business with his partner Emil Blumenau. After serving as a wireless operator in the German Air Force during the First World War he joined the business together with Emil Blumenau's son, also Hans. In 1936, as the plight of Jews in Germany worsened, Hans Blumenau came to London and established a factory in the King's Cross area under the name of Corsets Silhouette. In 1938 he 'sponsored' his friend Hans Lobbenberg and his family to leave Germany and join him; they lived in Edgware. Nine months after their arrival Hans Lobbenberg and his second wife, **Annemarie (Plot 12)** (née Rabl) had a son, Peter (now living in London and working as a forensic chartered accountant). Hans and Annemarie had married in 1934. She was born in 1908 in Carlsbad in Austrian Bohemia (later Czechoslovakia; now Karlovy Vary in the Czech Republic) and they had met through a mutual interest in bridge.

At the beginning of the Blitz the company was offered relocation to either Coventry or Shrewsbury. Shrewsbury was chosen and and the two Hanses

*The church hall in Tankerville Street, original home
of the Silhouette factory in Shrewsbury*

were grateful for their decision later, when huge damage was also caused to Coventry by German bombers. A new Silhouette factory therefore opened in fairly humble surroundings in a church hall in Tankerville Street (still there), later moving to Coton Hill. The business was successful and in the 1950s needed to move to larger premises; a brand new factory was therefore commissioned in Harlescott Lane, Shrewsbury. Construction was still underway when Hans Lobbenberg died aged 59 in 1955. As an employer he had always taken an old-fashioned paternal approach to his staff. He was truly 'loved by all' and made it his business to get to know each of his employees, remembering such things as their children's birthdays and sharing in their joys and sorrows.

Shortly after the War Hans Blumenau and his family moved back to London to re-establish the King's Cross factory. Whilst in Shrewsbury, the two families had lived together in a large house on Berwick Road known as Burnell House. With their extended families, as many as twelve people occupied the house at the same time. Hans Blumenau was something of a connoisseur of classical music and brought numerous famous soloists to the town to perform in the Lion Hotel on Wyle Cop. Whilst in Shrewsbury, these celebrities would invariably stay with the two families in Berwick Road.

When Hans Lobbenberg came to the county, he brought with him both a passion for and expertise in the game of chess. In the early post-War years he became something of a force in Shropshire chess circles, represented the county and won the Shropshire championship at his first attempt in 1947/48. On his way to the championship he beat the holder, Mr D. MacNab, in the

The old Silhouette factory in Harlescott Lane

semi-final, and clinched the title against another well-known local player of the time, J.H. Thomasson. Both finalists had founded businesses in the county town, as the defeated finalist ran the small electrical business of Thomasson and Holland in Barker Street. Hans Lobbenberg also knew and played against World Champion Emmanuel Lasker and Grand Master Fritz Saemisch — the latter being Best Man at his second marriage to Annemarie. Although not outwardly flamboyant, Lobbenberg did have a somewhat exotic taste in cars and could be seen around the streets of Shrewsbury initially in a 1938 Buick, which he later traded in for a Chevrolet and then a Studebaker.

His widow, Annemarie, had become involved in the Silhouette business as its Design Director, and was responsible for the design of the hugely successful 'Little-X' girdle. In 1948, **George Lobbenberg (Plot 12),** Hans' son by his first marriage, also joined the company as joint MD. He had been educated first in

Burnell House, Berwick Road, once home to both the Lobbenberg and Blumenau families

Switzerland and later in the United States, where his mother had gone to live. After service as a GI in Luxembourg with General Patton's army, he had returned to the USA to study journalism before joining his father in the UK. After Hans Lobbenberg's death in 1955, the company 'went public' though the Lobbenberg and Blumenau families still retained overall control. The company was by then flourishing and new satellite factories were opened in Market Drayton, Telford and Wem.

Production-line corset manufacture requires a large open space and to achieve this at the Market Drayton base George commissioned a building involving a particularly innovative use of laminated timber engineering. It consisted of eight 'hyperbolic paraboloid' timber shell roofs covering an open area of 120' by 240' and supported on a single central pillar. George had been impressed by an earlier factory in Wilton designed by Robert Townsend and hired him in 1959 to undertake the Market Drayton factory. The Wilton structure has now disappeared and, although the Silhouette building in Market Drayton was recently added to the 'list of buildings of special architectural or historical interest', it has also now been demolished and replaced by a supermarket, much to the disappointment of the Twentieth Century Society which had campaigned for its retention as a building of particular merit.

The Silhouette business was by then at its peak, close to a thousand people were in its employment and in Shrewsbury it was the second largest employer, after Rolls Royce's Sentinel works. Annemarie Lobbenberg died in 1971, preceded a year earlier by her step-son George who sadly, like his father, died at a relatively young age. His gravestone bears the legend 'Shalom my love'. After his death, Hans Blumenau's son Tom became sole MD so that the Lobbenberg/Blumenau partnership endured through three generations of both families. Sadly, the name of Silhouette was to disappear from the local and national business scene in somewhat unfortunate circumstances. In 1980 the company was sold to W.L. Pawson which went into receivership not long afterwards, depriving the town of several hundred jobs. Today, the Harlescott Lane premises are occupied by BT.

Hans, George and Annmarie Lobbenberg are buried at the top end of the 1939 extension to the Cemetery, close to a number of other members of Silhouette staff, in an area still known within the family as 'Silhouette corner'.

9   SHREWSBURY SCHOOL CONNECTIONS

The gravestone of **John Milns West (162)** stands in the lower part of Shrewsbury Cemetery not far from the eastern boundary. The inscription is brief but telling: 'John Milns West Soldier-Scholar-Servant. Knight of St John. 1897–1973'.

West was educated at Shrewsbury School and Kings College, Cambridge where he was a Choral Scholar. He joined the staff of Shrewsbury School in 1922 and served as a Master there for some 35 years. He was Housemaster of the School's day-boys from 1932 to '39 and then of Ingram's House from 1945 until his retirement; he also served on the School's governing body. Colonel West saw service in both Wars. During the First World War he was with the Rifle Brigade and served with the Royal Welch Fusiliers in the Second. It was perhaps not surprising therefore that in peacetime he took a great interest in the School Cadet Force, taking control of the Cadets from A.H. Pearson, at a time, in the early 1930s, when morale, it was said, was not high and standards had slipped. It was West's job to raise them both, and in this he seems to have succeeded.

D.J.V. Bevan, in his book *Recollections – a Shrewsbury Scrapbook* says: 'I remember once as we were marching back to the tea RV [rendezvous] at Church Stretton after a Field Day, the Platoon Commander of Oldham's [one of the school's 'houses'], who was with me, observed, 'Surely, Sir, this is the Corps to end Corps'. West's achievement was to smarten up the officers and create a certain self-respect if not keenness, among the cadets though this was not easy and took some time.' By the mid 1930s, the reputation and efficiency of the Corps had improved considerably.

West also cultivated an interest in the history of the School. In 1934 he collaborated with W.J. Pendlebury to produce a small volume entitled *Shrewsbury School – recent years*. Three years later this was followed by a more comprehensive history which he called simply *Shrewsbury* and which was entirely his own work. In a generous foreword, C.A. Alington, a well-known past headmaster of the School, wrote, 'I cannot claim to have taught Major West history: I wish I could for his learning fills me with admiration.'

West's self-effacing Preface speaks of the imperfections of 'this little book' and its many omissions, 'which Salopians will be quick to perceive.'

His colleague Basil Oldham, a man with a sometimes withering and acerbic view of others weaknesses, was not inclined to disagree. He wrote to a friend: 'Have you seen James [sic] West's book? It is much less inaccurate than I expected (though e.g. he gets one event 180 years wrong!) but it is not a serious, scholarly contribution to knowledge.' Some time earlier, when West produced a supplementary volume to the School Register, Oldham had rather gleefully kept a note of the mistakes, which ran into three figures. He was also critical when West, as editor of the *Salopian Newsletter*, made a mistake in his Honours column ('Do you see that ... West has given Carbonell the garter?!'). In 1952, to mark the fourth centenary of the School, Oldham wrote his own carefully researched and scholarly history, feeling no doubt that it was about time he showed West how the job should be done.

West's interests were not confined, however, to the somewhat closeted world of School life. He also had a long and active involvement in the civic life of his adopted town. He was first elected to the Town Council in 1930 as Conservative member for Kingsland ward. He was also to become chairman of the Water Committee and later was much in the public eye as chairman of the powerful and influential Highways and Planning committee. He served also as Education Adviser to the Council and as a Visitor at Shrewsbury Prison.

His long service on the Council was recognised in 1949 when he became an Alderman and later in 1952 when he was elected Mayor for the coming year. It was an apposite appointment, coming as it did in the year Shrewsbury School celebrated the 400th anniversary of the granting of its charter. His wife, Katherine, supported him as his Mayoress; she was a native of Canada and they had married in Toronto in 1934.

The anniversary celebrations, in June 1952, began with a presentation of the masque *Callover*, especially written for the occasion by dramatist Paul Dehn, himself an ex-pupil of the School. On 20 June a grand dinner for Old Salopians was held at the Music Hall, but was over-subscribed and the Lion Hotel had to accommodate the over-flow. The day before, Sir Offley Wakeman (chairman of the School governers) presented a new High Cross to the town; in a neat about-turn, it was received on the town's behalf by the Mayor, John West. The new Cross was placed at the top of Pride Hill following on from one erected to mark the 500th anniversary, in 1903, of the Battle of Shrewsbury. This had not survived long however being made of plaster and 'not so solid as it looked'. An inscription on the new Cross read: 'The Royal School of Shrewsbury presents [the Cross] to the town it loves. It changed its site but not its loyalty.' This was a reference to the School's move from its original site opposite the Castle to a new spacious one across the river in Kingsland.

The celebrations continued with a special Ceremony of Commemoration at the School, when the main speaker was Viscount Tedder, Chancellor of Cambridge University. The undoubted highlight and climax, however, was a visit in October by Queen Elizabeth and the Duke of Edinburgh, who visited the School and opened a new terrace overlooking the River Severn. To mark this occasion, the headmaster announced that three days were to be added to that year's Christmas holiday. At Shrewsbury station a proud Mayor officially bid the royal couple farewell on behalf of the School and the town.

Edward Branthwaite Moser (70) was born on 9 October 1850 at Kendal. He was destined, however, to spend the vast majority of his long life in Shrewsbury. Educated initially at Windermere College, he came to Shrewsbury School as a boarder in 1864. He proved to be a first rate scholar and sportsman, becoming captain of boating, captain of the football team for three successive seasons and 'huntsman' (head runner). From Shrewsbury he went on to become one of the leading classical scholars of his generation at St John's College, Cambridge.

In 1875, at the age of 25, he joined the staff of his old school in Shrewsbury and was to remain there for 36 years until his retirement in 1911. He then returned in 1915 and continued teaching throughout the First World War. He was said to be a fine teacher who took a personal interest in the education of each of his pupils. Moser also continued his interest in sporting matters and was instrumental in the establishment of the School's Boat Club, to which he donated boats, and took responsibility for coaching. Outside school he was a keen mountaineer in his younger days and a member of the Alpine Club.

His active interest in the School's sporting prowess continued after retirement, and right up to his death in 1936 his frail but upright figure could be seen regularly down at the river casting a critical eye over the School 'eight' as they rowed various courses before departing for Henley. Similarly, hardly a football or cricket match was played but he was there to appraise or blame. Moser's lifelong devotion to his invalid sister was great and he would note down every detail of a match on an envelope to report to her on his return. There was a lot more to him than the rather austere front that he presented to the world. In the words of John Milns West in his book *Shrewsbury*: 'His tongue could be somewhat bitter and withering at times but all with whom he came in contact realised — sometimes practically — the generous and kind heart which beat beneath 'The Captain's' stiff white shirt front' (Moser was always known within the School as either 'The Skipper' or 'The Captain').

Moser's time at Shrewsbury School as both a pupil and Master spanned that of three headmasters: Dr B.H. Kennedy (1836–66), Preb H.W. Moss (1866–1908) and C.A. Alington (1908–16). Towards the end of Prebendary Moss's time as headmaster, the School was at a low ebb and the number of pupils had fallen to only 230. Moss himself was by then an elderly man and amongst his Housemasters, the average length of service in the School was 27 years. Of those who had done most to establish the School at its new Kingsland site, after the move in 1882, Moser himself and Arthur Chance were both well into their 50s; the most junior Housemaster, 'Johnny' Baker, had been on the staff for 21 years and none of the Housemasters had ever taught at any other school. Moser and Chance were close friends, both were bachelors, both classical scholars and both Old Salopians. They were utterly devoted to the School and when C.A. Alington arrived as a new headmaster bringing with him a 'wind of change' they did not shirk from the challenges this presented.

Moser had a keen wit and a sometimes acerbic turn of phrase. Many of his sayings passed into School folklore. Once, at a musical entertainment there, a lady singer (of whose 'talent' Moser was not an admirer) was vociferously applauded. Turning to a neighbour, Moser remarked: 'If the silly fellows clap like that, they deserve to have her sing again.'

On 5 December 1905, disaster struck. During the second lesson of the day 'Top Schools' was found to be ablaze. The flames spread quickly until the whole roof collapsed. This included the clock tower, which struck 24 times until, melted by the intense heat, it toppled over and fell into the burning buildings. One of the masters' children was then seen to burst into tears and exclaim: 'Oh look, the poor clock is dying! It's dying!' T.E. Pickering, the librarian, anxious for the safety of his treasured tomes, could not be induced

The fire at Shrewsbury School on 5 December 1905:
the top floor well and truly ablaze,

to leave the burning building in spite of repeated attempts at persuasion. When Moser went to try and persuade Pickering out he received, for his trouble, a kick in the shin from an excited colleague, F.E. Bennett, who was there with the same intention. 'Then let the brute burn', ejaculated Moser in exasperation, though he continued his efforts to secure Pickering's safety which were ultimately successful.

After the fire, the decision was made to erect a new library building. A site was chosen next to the School science rooms and plans drawn up for a combined library, reading room and an area in which to display a valuable collection of nearly 80 English watercolours which Moser had announced he was to donate to the School. It was decided, as a mark of appreciation for his generous gesture, that the new building would bear his name. It still does so, as does the house which he had built near the school grounds (a not uncommon practice at the time) for the accommodation of boarders and of which he was Housemaster. The foundation stone of the Moser library building was laid by King George V when he visited the Royal Show held at Shrewsbury in July 1914. The project continued despite wartime stringencies and was opened in 1916 by a Cabinet Minister, Lord Milner, who was said to have looked thoroughly bored throughout the whole affair.

In September 1911, on his retirement, a presentation was made to Moser and his sister at the premises of Messrs Adnitt and Naunton in The Square. The tradesmen of the town gave them a silver revolving breakfast dish as well as a blotter inscribed with the names of the subscribers, as a 'momento of the happy business relations which had prevailed for many years.' The Mosers had always lived and shopped in the town and intended to continue doing so. This was obviously appreciated by Shrewsbury's shopkeepers.

Moser died in 1936 at the age of 85. The first paragraph of his obituary in *The Salopian*, a magazine for old boys of the School, read: 'No school can have been more fortunate than Shrewsbury in finding some of its sons willing, not merely to contribute of their substance to its welfare, but to donate their entire lives to its prosperity and progress. Such a one par excellence was Edward Branthwaite Moser whose whole heart was wrapped up in the activities and interests of his old school.' His funeral service was held in the School chapel where his coffin was draped in the

The Moser Library

Branthwaite House
built at Moser's expense to
house boarders from the school

School flag and he was buried at Shrewsbury Cemetery.

Henry Whitehead Moss (198) was one of a famous trio of 19th-century Headmasters at Shrewsbury. The trio were: Samuel Butler (1798–1836), Benjamin Hall Kennedy (1836–66) and Moss himself (1866–1908). He was Headmaster for longer than either Butler or Kennedy and his achievement in successfully moving the School to Kingsland certainly means he should be given equality of eminence with them. Moss however had a somewhat colder personality than his two predecessors. Nevertheless, even if he failed to inspire affection, he earned respect for his scholarship, integrity and devotion to the School.

Moss certainly had a sense of humour, albeit a rather ponderous one. A rather darker side to his character, however, emerged when he flogged the son of **John Loxdale (181)** 88 times for bringing ale into his study. This led to an inquiry by the Governors and no little controversy. Moss's career as Headmaster nevertheless survived this unsavoury incident, though it may explain why, despite being a Prebendary of Hereford, he was never offered a Bishopric. As a scholar, he excelled at classics and was almost equally as good at mathematics and read to such an extent that he strained his eyes and had to wear spectacles. He did not participate in sports, preferring long walks instead. Moss went to Shrewsbury School at 16 and became as devoted to the then Headmaster, Dr Kennedy, as Kennedy had been to Butler. After achieving scholarly excellence again at Cambridge, he was appointed Headmaster of Shrewsbury in 1866, having only just been ordained and aged only 24.

Moss brought with him a plan which only a young man could have the energy and courage to carry through. Some years earlier, in 1861, a Royal Commission had been established to enquire into the 'endowments, funds and revenues' of certain public schools. One outcome of the Commission's report was the Public Schools Act of 1868 which introduced the idea of Governing Bodies. The report was generally favourable in relation to Shrewsbury but did recommend an increase and improvement of the accommodation. Moss, realising that expansion of the Castle Gates site would be well nigh impossible, saw the recommendation as an enormous opportunity. Immediately upon his appointment he aired the idea of purchasing a new and larger site on the outskirts of the town. Nevertheless, it was eight years later, in 1874, before the Governors finally decided that Shrewsbury Corporation should be invited to sell them the 18th-century House of Industry on Kingsland, along with 27 acres of adjoining land.

The intervening years had been filled with controversy. Public meetings were held, newspaper articles and pamphlets written and a petition of 600 names (Old Salopians and townsfolk) opposing the move was collected; businessmen in the town feared it would mean lost trade as well as making it more difficult for their sons to attend the School. Despite this, a scheme slowly developed and progressed. The first site proposed was on high ground beyond Coton Hill, but it was soon realised that whenever the Severn flooded the approach to Coton Hill, access would effectively be cut off. Briefly, a site next to the General Cemetery was considered. However, when Moss was walking over the area one day, musing on its suitability, he observed at least six funerals arrive and decided against it. Attention then shifted to the Kingsland site which was finally acquired in 1876, and gradually new buildings arose to receive the School. The opening day in 1882 was marked by special services at St Mary's and a luncheon in the Corn Exchange, after which a Band led a procession over the new toll bridge up to the new school and a ceremonial opening in a large marquee.

This achievement was undoubtedly Moss's main claim to lasting fame, but he achieved much more during his 42 years as Headmaster. Although not a games-player himself, he presented the School with a swimming-bath as a personal gift and bought six acres of land (which he later sold to the School for a lesser sum) to expand the playing fields. He revived Speech Day, re-established the Rifle Corps and provided for the teaching of mathematics and, after some delay, of modern languages and natural sciences. One singular innovation was the introduction of Merit Halves — a half day's holiday given as a reward for academic achievement, punctuality in chapel, and a minimal number of punishments.

Moss retired in 1908, handing the reins to C.A. Alington, whose short-lived but enigmatic tenure of the post introduced a new and modern era for the School. Moss lived in Oxford for nine years after retirement and when he died on 14 January 1917 was buried in Shrewsbury Cemetery. The grave was described later by his wife as being 'within the sound of the School bell and the cheers from the football field' After the War, a committee was established to create a suitable memorial for him. As a result, the main School gates were removed to the Port Hill entrance and replaced by 'more dignified' ones (designed by W.A. Forsyth). These were formally opened by Mrs Moss in May 1923. The inscription on the gates gives him the latinised name of Henrico and it was this by which he was known for many years after.

Frederick Barnwell (168) was also a long-serving employee of Shrewsbury School, though not on the teaching staff. His gravestone in the Cemetery reads: 'This monument was erected by the Masters and boys of Shrewsbury School in memory of Frederick George Barnwell who died 22 April 1924 aged 67 and in grateful appreciation of his 32 years faithful service.'

Barnwell served the School initially as Tuck Shop manager and later as Porter and Caretaker. He had a military background and joined the 7th Company of the Shropshire Rifle Volunteers in 1877, continuing his service in the 1st Volunteer Battalion of the King's Shropshire Light Infantry until 1909. After the re-organisation of the Volunteer Battalions into the modern Territorial Army, he retired after 32 years' service with the rank of Colour Sergeant, which he had held for seven years. Barnwell had a well-earned reputation as an excellent shot and won the Shrewsbury Company shooting cup for five years in succession. On retirement he was presented with an illuminated address signed by Captain G.G. Wace, his commanding officer.

Appropriately, Barnwell was given a full military funeral. His coffin was accompanied by the Band of the 4th KSLI and a detachment of the same Battalion brought up the rear. Amongst the mourners were his five sons who all saw service with the King's Shropshire Light Infantry in the First World War.

The Moss Gates with, above, a detail of the dedication to
Henry Whitehead Moss

10   FOOTBALLING HEROES

One of the true surprises of Shrewsbury Cemetery is the number of illustrious footballers who lie buried there. Many rose to fame in the early days of organised football, but the story is one that continues right up to the present day.

John Hawley Edwards (56) was one of the foremost pioneers of soccer in the border counties in the 1870s and for good reason he became known as the 'godfather of Shropshire football'. As a player, he was a great exponent of the old fashioned dribbling game, his only weakness, according to the *Shrewsbury Chronicle*, being that he 'prefers a crooked course to a straight one.' During a glittering career, he became one of the select band of players capped by both England and Wales and scored in an FA Cup Final.

Born in March 1850, he founded and captained a team of gentleman amateur players known as the Shropshire Wanderers, which reached the FA Cup semi-finals in 1875. He also played for the more illustrious Wanderers team from London, for whom he appeared in the 1876 Cup Final at Kennington Oval. It took two games to settle the tie. The first, played in a howling gale, ended 1–1 with Edwards opening the scoring for Wanderers after 35 minutes, only for Alex Bonsor to equalise for Old Etonians five minutes into the second half. *The Sportsman* newspaper described Edwards' goal as follows: 'For nearly half an hour the Etonians kept their opponents at bay, but at last Wollaston getting the ball cleverly past Thompson, took it into the centre and thence Hawley Edwards, by a cleverly directed kick, shot it just under the bar of the Eton goal.' The replay produced a convincing 3–0 victory for the Wanderers team and the first of three successive FA Cup wins.

Playing for the Old Etonians in both matches was another Salopian, Captain W.S. Kenyon-Slaney. Ironically, Kenyon-Slaney had earlier, in 1873, been an FA Cup winner with the same Wanderers team from London now represented by Hawley Edwards.

By the time of his Cup Final appearance Edwards had already represented England when he was called up as a late replacement for J.G. Wylie in a friendly match against Scotland on 7 March 1874. The game took place at the West of Scotland Cricket Ground, Glasgow, attracted a crowd of 7,000 and resulted in a 2–1 win for the home side. The press of the time reported that Edwards had an excellent match, 'in spite of the disadvantages under which he laboured from being a stranger to most of his own team.' At the time of his appearance for England, the Welsh FA had not been founded. When it was, Edwards became its first treasurer as well as playing for the Welsh national side in its very first match — another friendly against Scotland at the West of Scotland Cricket Ground. This game took place on 25 March 1876, shortly before Edwards' FA Cup triumph. It attracted a substantial crowd of some 17,000 and resulted in an emphatic 4–0 win for Scotland.

Edwards was born in Shrewsbury where his family lived on Pride Hill. It seems, however, that as he was involved in the formation of the FA of Wales, and then in running it, there was no one able to challenge him over his qualification to play for Wales. This would have been further confused by the close involvement of many Shropshire clubs in Welsh football.

Edwards was to return to his Welsh border roots for the start of the 1876/77 season. His footballing reputation in the area was such that an attempt by the Druids team to bolster their ranks by including him under the false name of Jones, had once caused much ill-feeling and controversy among their opponents Wrexham. Edwards added to his reputation by captaining the Shrewsbury Town side which won both the Birmingham Senior Cup and the Shropshire FA Cup in 1877/78, and continued playing for a further two years until he was forced to retire due to a series of knee injuries.

Professionally he had followed in his father's footsteps and was admitted as a solicitor in 1871 and served as Clerk to Shrewsbury Magistrates for 19 years. He also played an active role in the administration of the game. As well as being the Welsh FA's first Treasurer, he had a spell on the committee of the Birmingham and District FA and was a member of the founding committee of the Shropshire FA in 1877.

Although football was undoubtedly his first love, Edwards was also an accomplished cricketer. He played for Shropshire from 1867 to 1876, Warwickshire (though not 'first class') and Shrewsbury Cricket Club. In later years he also became a keen angler. His early death at the age of only 42, on 14 January 1893, came as a result of a throat infection while he was staying at Old Colwyn, Denbighshire.

John Charles Henry Bowdler (134), known variously as Jack and Charlie, was educated at Shrewsbury School, where his prodigious sporting talents soon came to the fore and he became School captain of football as well as 'huntsman' (or captain of running). At the tender age of 15 he helped to form and played for the first Shrewsbury Town team. This, however, led to some criticism for 'divided loyalties' and according to a contemporary edition of *The Salopian* magazine he 'learned nothing' from his experiences with the town club. The young Bowdler could perform equally well on either wing or at inside forward, had speed, good ball control and packed a strong shot. In October 1887, Shrewsbury Town won their first FA Cup tie at Macclesfield. Bowdler, still a schoolboy, travelled by train and arrived late, 'but the moment he stepped on the field he seized the ball and, making straight for goal, scored.' The match was won 3–1 thanks largely to his skill and determination.

J.C.H. Bowdler

These skills were also recognised at an international level and he had the opportunity to play for Wales whilst still at school. He was unable to take up the offer then but made up for this in 1890 when he gained his first Welsh cap against Ireland. The match was played on 8 February 1890 at the Monkmoor Racecourse ground in Shrewsbury and remains the only full international match ever to have been played in Shropshire. The night before the game the Irish contingent was entertained at an 'invitation smoking concert' held at the Crown Hotel (next to St Mary's church). Shrewsbury Gymnasium Club gave displays of dumbbells and boxing

The Wales team that played Ireland in 1890; J.C.H. Bowlder is seated far right

and Bowdler and another new cap, goalkeeper S.G. Gillam, 'sang ditties as part of the frivolity'. Wales won the match 5–2 in front of a crowd of 4,000 and Bowdler went on to win a further four caps over the following five years, scoring a total of three goals. He was technically not eligible to play for Wales having been born in Shrewsbury, but the Welsh FA conveniently recorded his birthplace as Llandrindod Wells in their record books.

Bowdler left Shrewsbury Town in 1890 and had spells with Wolverhampton Wanderers and Blackburn Rovers, becoming the first Old Boy of Shrewsbury School to play League football. He appeared in two FA Cup semi-finals (though by a cruel twist of fate, playing for Wolves in the year Blackburn won the Cup and vice-versa) and clocked up over 50 League and FA Cup appearances. Although an amateur throughout his career, it was not uncommon at the time for banknotes to be found in player's boots at the end of a game. The amount depended on the quality of the player's performance and Bowdler's spell in the Football League proved financially profitable. He returned to Shrewsbury in 1893 to play for the Town again and used the money he had earned to qualify as a solicitor. He served his articles partly with John Hawley Edwards, another local footballing stalwart, and partly with H.W. Hughes of Castle Street, the largest firm of solicitors in the town at the time.

Once qualified, he set up his own firm which became J.C.H. Bowdler and Son when his son Charles later joined him. The firm remained prominent in the commercial landscape of Shrewsbury until 1988 when part of it merged with Lanyon's to become Lanyon Bowdler. The remainder of the original firm continued under the name of John Bowdler's and is still run today by the founder's grandson, Mr John Bowdler.

Despite a fruitless attempt by Blackburn to re-sign him in 1895, J.C.H. Bowdler remained in Shrewsbury playing for the local club. He also went on to serve Shrewsbury Town as Secretary and Chairman. It was a time when the Club was often struggling financially and on many occasions he was forced to utilise his political and other connections in order to keep the Club afloat. It is said that in 1901 he used his own money to keep the Club going for a whole month.

In later years Bowdler became a more than useful bowls player for the Severnside club and represented Shropshire many times in inter-county matches. He also served for many years as Tory councillor for Belle Vue on Shrewsbury Town Council. His death came at the age of only 57. He had been to see the doctor because of severe indigestion and was advised that he needed more exercise. As a result, he began to undertake regular ten mile hikes but on 18 July 1927 collapsed and died after one of these walks.

J.C.H.'s brother **Harry Ernest Bowdler (148)** was also a footballer of considerable renown. They are said between them to have played a part in establishing the original Shrewsbury Town football club, whilst both were still at Shrewsbury School. Unlike his brother, however, Ernie never played in the Football League, though he did achieve one Welsh cap whilst a Shrewsbury Town player. He was a clever winger but had little chance to shine as Wales went down 8–0 to Scotland in 1891. Nevertheless, in a forward line which also included his brother J.C.H. Bowdler on the opposite wing, he was said in match reports to be the fastest and 'best in front of goal'.

Ernie hit the local headlines at the end of the 1892/93 season when, in the final League game at home to St George's, play came to an end 15 minutes early due to a pitch invasion. This occurred, according to contemporary reports, after Fowler — the visitors' right back — kicked out at Bowdler and his father went on to the pitch to remonstrate with the errant defender! Ernie continued to play locally for Shrewsbury Town until 1901 and, like his father and brother before him, joined the legal profession and held several public appointments in the town. He died at the early age of 48 from appendicitis and was buried in a section of Shrewsbury Cemetery just east of the Chapel and near to other members of the Bowdler family.

Another man from the Shrewsbury area who rose to prominence in the early days of football was **Clopton Allen Lloyd Jones (147)** (the last two names are sometimes hyphenated but were not on his birth certificate). In the 1880 FA Cup final, with just ten minutes to go and much against the run of play, Clopton broke through the Oxford University defence and scored for his team, Clapham Rovers, in front of a record crowd of 6,000. Oxford students who had travelled to Kennington Oval for the game could only watch, almost in disbelief, as Clapham hung on to their lead to become only the fifth club to have their name inscribed on the famous trophy.

Lloyd Jones' club, Clapham Rovers, had been formed in 1869. Among the earliest members of the Football Association, the club was one of fifteen teams to compete in the very first FA Cup competition in 1872. The early years of the FA Cup were dominated by four teams — Wanderers, Royal Engineers, Old Etonians and Oxford University. In 1873/74 Clapham had reached the semi-final stage, but then had a number of disappointing years. In 1878/79 their fortunes revived with the arrival of a number of new players including Clopton Allen Lloyd Jones and in 1880, thanks to his late goal, they became the first club outside the 'big four' to win the FA Cup. A contemporary newspaper report of the Final recorded the scene:

> Lloyd Jones scored for Clapham Rovers to 'vociferous cheers' after a good run by Sparks. The applause for Clapham Rovers' play indicated that they were the popular party, the plucky manner in which they have fought for the Cup since its inception and the hard luck they have had on more than one occasion justifying the feeling in their favour.

The Sportsman recorded that Lloyd Jones' goal for Clapham was greeted by, 'vociferous cheering, throwing up of hats and other demonstrations of delight from their supporters.'

In 1884, he returned to Shropshire and, after a brief spell playing for Pontesbury, joined the Shrewsbury Castle Blues. The Blues, however, disbanded in 1886 after a number of its players were found guilty of 'violent and dangerous play' and Clopton's active footballing career effectively ended with them. It was a highly successful career during which he had represented London, Middlesex, Surrey and Shropshire, as well as being selected for Wales against England during the 1884/85 season, though he was not available to take his place in the Welsh line-up. He was also a keen cricketer and represented Herefordshire, Shropshire and Radnorshire after his footballing career had ended.

Being an amateur player, he worked as an Indigo Broker in London and as a Commission Agent (or bookmaker) when he returned to Shrewsbury. He had been born in 1858 at Hanwood House (now demolished) in the village of the same name. Between 1891 and 1894 he is recorded as living at Claremont Bank, Darwin Cottage, The Mount from 1895 to 1902 and then Montreux, Belle Vue Gardens where he died in 1918 of cancer of the bladder (after a 'long and painful illness'). His obituary in the *Shrewsbury Chronicle* records that he was a prominent member of the Pengwern Boat Club and a keen supporter of Severnside Bowling Club in his later years, but makes no mention at all of his footballing exploits. He left a widow (Catherine, also known as Lily, whom he married in 1894) and four children. Their youngest son was given his father's name of Clopton.

Clopton snr was buried in Shrewsbury Cemetery, near to the graves of the two Bowdler brothers. His gravestone bears the Italian motto *Godi Tu Che Vinci* which roughly translates as 'Enjoy, you who win'. His father (who was known as the Squire of Hanwood) was buried in Hanwood churchyard and there is a plaque inside the church there to the memory of his son. His mother, **Margaret Lloyd Jones (147)** however was laid to rest in Shrewsbury Cemetery. When he died, the gross value of his estate was only £2,444 and the net value, after debts had been paid, was reportedly nil. Clopton's brother, Charles Frederick, however, appears to have accepted responsibility for Clopton's widow and in his will left her an income of £300 a year from the rent charges on his family estates.

Captain of Shrewsbury Castle Blues in 1884 when Lloyd Jones joined the club was **John Woodhouse Thatcher (105)**. Thatcher was headmaster of Hanwood School at the time and, as the village was also the Lloyd Jones family home, may well have been instrumental in persuading him to do so. Thatcher remained captain of the club until it disbanded. He also played three times for Shropshire, against Staffordshire, Denbighshire and Herefordshire, as a centre or half back.

The Blues were formed in the 1870s by a group of friends in Shrewsbury. By the time Thatcher joined them they had graduated from playing neighbouring clubs in the town to taking on clubs from elsewhere in Shropshire, Staffordshire and over the border in Wales. In April 1883 he played for them when they won the Wrekin Challenge Cup by beating Market Drayton 3–2. The *Shrewsbury Chronicle* described him as one of 'the best of the backs' when the Blues faced Wellington Town at Underdale recreation ground, Monkmoor the same month. Wellington won 1–0 though the Blues unsuccessfully appealed against the result, alleging that the ball had been handled into their goal.

Twelve months later, by which time Thatcher had become captain, the tables were turned. In the 1884 final of the County Cup they faced Wellington three times. The first two matches, at Underdale and Eyton (near Wellington), ended goal-less, before the next replay saw Blues winning 2–1 at Underdale. This caused much resentment amongst Wellington supporters who, under various pen-names such as 'FAIRPLAY', wrote bitter letters to the *Wellington Journal and Shrewsbury News* accusing the Blues of rough play. This was refuted by 'J.W. THATCHER, Captain of the Blues' who wrote:

> FAIRPLAY ought to have been one of the umpires or rather referee, and then perhaps Wellington would have had <u>fairplay</u>, as he makes out that they had anything but that ... They [all the writers] also assert that seven out of the eleven were kicked and bruised to a very great extent ... Now SCARROTT'S injuries were not from brutal play but from over-exertion. I walked up with him from the field to the hotel and he only complained that it was too long to play. MEREDITH received his injuries not in any of the matches against the Blues, but in previous matches. 'Fairplay' and 'Vigilant' have not so far forgotten themselves in the meanwhile to ask how it has fared with the Blues in these matches and throughout the season. We have had more men hurt in matches than any other football club in Shropshire by our opponents' rough play.

The capture of the County Cup in 1884 was really the club's zenith. The following season saw a decline in its fortunes, beginning with the loss of the Cup to St George's, who won 2–0. Their final season (1885–86) saw allegations of rough play again come to the fore. Three Blues players were disciplined by the Birmingham Football Association after complaints over their play in a match against Saltley College. Further damage was done to their reputation by three Blues members who, as spectators, joined a pitch invasion and violent mêlée sparked by a dispute in a game between Castle Rovers and Wellington Town at the Comet Ground, Ditherington in January 1886. The three were arrested, convicted of assault and fined. The cumulative effect of all this controversy proved fatal to the club and the decision was taken to disband at the end of the season. It was following this decision that Shrewsbury Town was formed, at least partly as an attempt to revive Shrewsbury's footballing reputation.

Thatcher's time in charge of Hanwood School ended in 1885 and after the demise of the Blues he seems to have concentrated on his teaching career. He had become a schoolmaster in Hertford, Essex when he returned to his father's home in Coton Hill to die aged only 27 on 4 January 1888, still unmarried. His grave, near the centre of the Cemetery, is unmarked but nearby is the headstone of his mother, **Mary Thatcher (105)** who died in 1876.

Occasional accidental injuries are an almost inevitable part of a game involving physical contact, such as football. Deaths arising from such injuries are, however, mercifully rare. Such was the fate, nevertheless, of a young Shrewsbury man in 1893. His gravestone in Shrewsbury Cemetery reads as follows: **'John Henry Morris (176)** who died 12th November 1893 (through accident in a football match) aged 23. This memorial was erected by his fellow players and friends in the Shrewsbury Town FC (with much sympathy).'

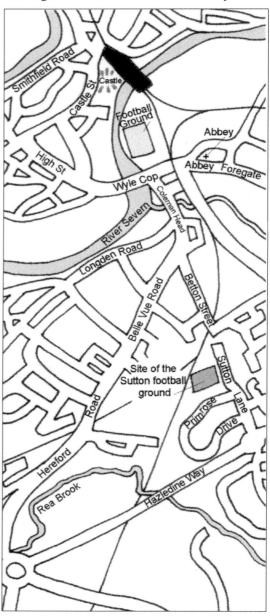

Map showing the likely location of Shrewbury Town's pitch at Sutton

100

John Morris (known as 'Jack'), a labourer in a brickyard, lived with his sister in Canal Buildings, New Park Road in Castlefields and was Shrewsbury Town's left back. The team at the time were playing at a ground in Sutton Lane. It was a short lived and not very successful venue being, at the time, some distance out of the town. On 11 November 1893, Shrewsbury were playing Madeley Town in the first round of the Wednesbury Charity Cup when Morris sustained his fatal injury. Madeley were already losing 4–0 when their outside left, William Evans, dribbled towards the Shrewsbury goal. Jack came across to clear the ball, the pair collided and he went down. 'Jack, are you much hurt?' enquired the Shrewsbury right back, Herbert Evers. Receiving only a groan in response, he ventured: 'It's a pity, I think it was purely accidental.' 'Oh no, Evers, it was done on purpose,' Morris replied.

He was carried to the dressing room and later taken to the Salop Infirmary (then behind St Mary's church). There was subsequently some confusion about what exactly happened there. Whatever the reason, Morris didn't want to stay. Allegedly, as he groaned in pain, he was told: 'Don't be a baby' and it was implied that if he had to return to the Infirmary he would not be treated.

He was taken, limping badly, to the Unicorn Hotel and given a drop of brandy and there repeated his accusation that his injuries had been caused deliberately. Later, when the pain persisted, he saw a doctor and returned to the Infirmary with a note saying that he should be admitted. Staff there debated whether or not to operate, but ultimately decided against it, preferring to arrange a further consultation the following day to see if the symptoms had become more urgent. A haemorrhage to the abdomen was diagnosed, but it was believed to have stopped bleeding; the possibility of a rupture was also raised but no specific symptoms could be found. Jack died of internal bleeding on 12 November, the day after the game.

An inquest was held at the Clarendon Hotel, Shrewsbury on the following day, and such was the interest that a large crowd gathered outside. The Coroner, **R.E. Clarke (132)**, admitted to the jury that, in the whole of his experience as a sportsman, he had never played football and could not therefore guide them on the rules. He went on, in a masterpiece of condescension, to say that: 'Football was a game in which a great deal of animosity might be shown either by the players personally or by the team as a whole, and it was also one of those games in which there was the chance of an amount of rough usage which would not take place when playing cricket or hockey.' Football was a lawful game he was prepared to concede but, 'proper caution must be exercised', otherwise a charge of manslaughter was not an impossibility.

Although present, Evans, the Madeley player, appears not to have given evidence but there seems to have been nothing in any of the testimony (including that of a watching policeman) to suggest the fatal clash had been anything other than a pure accident. The captain of Shrewsbury Town FC, J.C.H. Bowdler, explained some of the rules of the game to the jury — and no doubt the Coroner — including that putting the knee up in a tackle was not allowed. In his summing up, Coroner Clarke went to great pains to exonerate the Infirmary and its doctors from any blame whatsoever. Morris was treated most kindly there he said and 'could not be treated better anywhere.' Ultimately, and inevitably, the jury returned a verdict of accidental death. As Evans left, he was 'hooted by members of the crowd and it was found necessary to afford him police protection to the railway station.'

On the day of his funeral, a large crowd gathered to pay their final respects to Jack, a promising player who had turned out for Shropshire against Wolverhampton Wanderers at St George's only a few days before his death. As his coffin was conveyed from his home in Castlefields to the Cemetery, the streets were lined with spectators. The whole of the funeral expenses were met by the President of the Shrewsbury Town club, Mr H.D. Greene QC MP.

The link between Shrewsbury Cemetery and footballing legends has continued to the present day. **George Arthur Rowley (Plot 18)** is accurately described on his headstone as a 'record breaking football hero'. In a 19-year career, he scored 434 League goals, a British record which is unlikely ever to be broken. Of that total, 152 were scored as player-manager of Shrewsbury Town. For anyone who had the experience of standing on the terraces at Gay Meadow, watching Big Arthur's burly frame stampede through nervous defences was worth every penny of the admission fee. An opponent once summed up what it was like to play against him: 'I don't know how he does it. He's a big fellow, easy to see out of the corner of your eye and not particularly quick, but one second you're there with him and the next he's gone and he's shooting.'

Figures can only tell part of the story, but the statistics of his remarkable career make astonishing reading. He scored 251 goals in 301 games for Leicester City and 152 in 236 for Shrewsbury Town. He netted four goals in a match on two occasions and 24 hat-tricks. His tally included 52 penalties and he scored 20 or more goals in 13 consecutive seasons. His highest total in one season was 44 (in 42 games) for Leicester City, and he broke the Shrewsbury Town record with 38 in the 1958/59 season. Dixie Dean's goal scoring record was passed when he scored his 380th goal and in September 1962, in front of a crowd of 8,503 at Gay Meadow, he scored one of his best ever goals to beat the 24-year-old British record of Celtic's Jimmy McGrory; it was his 411th goal.

Arthur Rowley was born in Wolverhampton in 1927. By the late 1930s his skills became apparent when he was attending the local St Peter's Collegiate School. He gained a place in the Wolverhampton Schools team and played for Birmingham and Staffordshire. At 14 he was signed up by Manchester

United but moved to West Bromwich Albion when, after the War, he turned professional. His time at the Hawthorns brought him only four goals in 23 games. A transfer to Fulham resulted in 27 goals in 56 outings, followed by a move back to the Midlands when he joined Leicester City in 1951.

It was at City's Filbert Street ground that Rowley really established his goal-scoring prowess. He scored 28 goals in his first season there — his lowest seasonal total for the club. In eight seasons he was their top scorer. Playing at inside left, he twice broke the club's individual goal-scoring record and was once leading marksman in the whole Football League. He had helped Fulham to promotion in 1948/49 and played a massive part in twice getting Leicester back into the First Division (now the Premiership).

It was something of a surprise therefore when, at the age of 32, Leicester allowed Rowley to leave and take up the post of Shrewsbury Town's first player-manager. He was keen to move into management and had fond memories of the town from a time he had spent in the Army based at Copthorne Barracks. Over the next ten years he provided Town fans with a treasure trove of memories, both as a player and a manager. Renowned throughout the lower divisions for his powerful and accurate shooting, he played on through the pain barrier to the age of 39. Almost inevitably, he bowed out with a goal in his final game against Bournemouth on 24 May 1965. By a strange twist of fate, Arthur's final visit to the Meadow as a spectator, just five days before his death, was also for a game against Bournemouth.

In his first season as player-manager, he led Town to promotion to the old Third Division and as a manager had a remarkable eye for a player, making

George Arthur Rowley

some great signings for the club. These included players such as Peter Dolby, Alf Wood, Jimmy McLaughlin, Ted Hemsley and Frank Clarke as well as England international Peter Broadbent, a player he considered the finest ever to play for Shrewsbury Town. During his time, the club earned a reputation as doughty Cup fighters. Twice they reached the fifth round of the FA Cup, losing 2–0 away to Leeds United in 1965 and 3–2 to Chelsea at Stamford Bridge the following season. This latter game was played in front of a crowd of 51,144, the highest ever to watch Shrewsbury Town play.

Arthur finally left the Meadow in August 1968 after Shrewsbury had narrowly missed promotion to the old Second Division. He became manager of Sheffield United, a decision he was later to describe as his only regret in football. Leaving Sheffield in a strong financial position, he moved on again to manage Southend United. After leaving the Essex club, Arthur and his wife quickly made the decision to return to Shropshire where a short spell with Oswestry Town, and then Welsh club Knighton, ended his active involvement in the game. The pair settled down to a quiet life living in Copthorne and in his later years Arthur became a regular visitor to the Gay Meadow, rarely missing a home game. In 2000, to his obvious delight, he was voted Shrewsbury Town's 'player of the century', followed in second place by Alf Wood, one of his signings for the club. A year later he was interviewed for the 'Meadow Memories' video, which charted the first 50 years of League football at the Gay Meadow. Picking his words carefully, and always acknowledging the support he got from others, his final words were: 'that's something I appreciate more than anything else, that people still remember and stop me in the street and say "thanks for the memories and pleasure you gave us when you were here playing" .'

Arthur Rowley died on 18 December 2002 at the age of 76; he was laid to rest in Shrewsbury Cemetery at the traditional Saturday kick-off time of 3pm. On Boxing Day, a minute's silence was impeccably observed before Leicester's game against Ipswich at their new ground, the Walkers Stadium, and before the game between Bury and Shrewsbury Town at the Gay Meadow. The Town players paid him the perfect tribute by producing an impressive performance to run out 4–1 winners.

11 THE ULTIMATE SACRIFICE

Just inside the original entrance to Shrewsbury Cemetery stands the impressive Portland stone Cross of Sacrifice commemorating the dead of the First World War. Its design is a standard one by Sir Reginald Blomfield (also architect of the Menin Gate memorial in Belgium) and similar memorials can be seen in cemeteries throughout the country. The cross is inscribed:

TO THE
HONOURED MEMORY
OF THOSE
SAILORS AND SOLDIERS
WHO GAVE THEIR LIVES
IN THE GREAT WAR
1914-1918
AND WHO LIE BURIED
IN THIS CEMETERY
THEIR NAME LIVETH FOR EVERMORE

The Cross of Sacrifice

The Imperial (later Commonwealth) War Graves Commission was established by Royal Charter in 1917. Part of its aim was to mark war graves (primarily those in overseas war cemeteries) with headstones which in size and quality made no distinction between rank or class. When it came to marking graves in British cemeteries some families who could afford to do so had already erected gravestones of their chosen design. The majority however were marked with wooden crosses which the War Graves Commission headstones replaced when the War was over. The Commission's policy of providing headstones was a boon to many families. Previously, in the 19th century, ordinary soldiers were sometimes provided with headstones at the expense of their regimental comrades and officers, but large numbers were buried in unmarked 'common graves'. Most servicemen came from poor families to whom a private grave, let alone a gravestone, was beyond their meagre resources.

The headstones continued to be provided until 1921, when the registration of service graves by the Commission ceased (only to be revived after the outbreak of the Second World War). Circumstances of death were no bar to commemoration by the War Graves Commission, and the headstones provided dignity to those who died in institutions, at a time when mental illness still carried a great stigma. Six First World War soldiers who died at the County Asylum at Shelton are among those buried in Shrewsbury Cemetery. Equally, suicides and those who died from accidents or from disease at home received headstones as well as those who died 'a hero's death' in battle. At least 15 of those victims of the Great War buried in the Cemetery died in local hospitals from wounds received on the Western Front. Thousands of wounded servicemen were transported to Shrewsbury by train for treatment and convalescence at various institutions and locations. These included the old Royal Salop Infirmary (behind St Mary's church), 1 Quarry Place, 'Cyngfelde' in Kingsland, Baschurch Surgical Home and Wellington Cottage Hospital. Later, a war hospital was also established in the former Atcham Union workhouse at Cross Houses.

Most of the First World War graves are scattered throughout the old part of the Cemetery and are generally of men from local families. Many of the Roman Catholic servicemen (though not all) were buried in sections 50, 51 and 66. Otherwise the largest concentration is in the bottom, southern, end of the Cemetery in sections 192, 197 and 198 where ultimately 52 servicemen were buried.

The human carnage of the First World War — especially on the Western Front — can also be glimpsed in the numerous references on family gravestones to sons who were killed, died of wounds or simply went missing in action never to be found alive again. From early in the war the British government forbade the return of bodies to Britain, so such inscriptions do not indicate burial in the Cemetery only that the families wished their sons to be remembered here in Shrewsbury. Records show, however, that all of them were buried in war cemeteries abroad, or are listed on special memorials to the missing. To give but a few examples:

Richard Edward Jones (118), twice Mayor of Shrewsbury, lost his only son **Major George Worthington Jones, MC (118)**, Commanding Officer of the Shropshire Royal Horse Artillery Battery, who died of wounds in a field hospital near Ypres in 1917. With his death the family's maltings business, founded by his Welsh grandfather, lost its heir, as he was childless though married. **Clement Clift (33)**, town councillor and painter and decorator, lost three sons, all of whom died of wounds in France in an 11 month period

106

between April 1917 and March 1918. **Joseph Winfield (210)** also lost three sons, in his case inside nine months — Ernest killed in action in France April 1918, Leslie (serving in the 4th King's Shropshire Light Infantry) died in France a week after the Armistice and middle son Alfred Victor, who had served in the Royal Engineers, died aged 26 in January 1919 having been invalided out of France and discharged in 1917.

Henry Makepeace Walton (207) not only lost a sailor son at the Battle of Jutland (1916) but also a son on the Western Front in 1917. **Samuel Atherton (134)** died in 1933 having had to sell the Hanwood colliery and brickyard which he owned, because his only son to reach manhood, Walter, a lieutenant in the 4th KSLI, was killed near Cambrai on 30 December 1917. Former Town Clerk and Coroner **H.C. Clarke (117)** died in 1917, a year after losing his eldest son, Colin, captain in the Army Service Corps, in an accident at the front. Colin had made a successful career as a solicitor and later barrister in Canada before joining up in the cause of his old country.

The youngest casualty of the Great War buried in Shrewsbury Cemetery is **Boy 2nd Class Henry George Price (21)**. Known as 'Rennie', he enlisted in the Royal Navy and was a member of the crew of *HMS Impregnable* when he was taken sick and died at his family home, 5 Burton Street, Castlefields, on 29 December 1914 at the age of 16. Only a matter of weeks later the aptly named **Private Alfred Edward Young (205)** died at the Military Isolation Hospital, Aldershot, on 4 February 1915. According to the Commonwealth War Graves Commission records he was aged 19, however the cemetery register states his age as 17. Like so many of his peers he seems to have lied about his age in order to enlist. He was one of many 'Shrewsbury Pals' who joined up soon after Lord Kitchener launched the system of 'Pals' battalions for county regiments. His home was in Bishop Street, Cherry Orchard, and he had been employed in Shropshire County Council's Local Taxation Department at the old Shirehall in The Square.

There are at least two First World War servicemen aged over 60 buried in the Cemetery. **Private James Dolman (192)**, Royal Defence Corps (RDC), died at his home in St Alkmund's Place on 13 March 1919 aged 61. He had entered the KSLI National Reserve in 1915 (later incorporated into the RDC). His family erected a headstone which also commemorates two sons who were both killed in action in 1915, and four others who also served as their father did. The oldest however appears to be **Private Joseph Peel (198)** also of the Royal Defence Corps who died of bronchitis on 15 April 1917 at Knockaloe Internment Camp, Patrick, Isle of Man, where he was stationed. His age — according to the Cemetery Register — was 67. Private Peel's home at the time of his death was 3 Ladysmith Terrace, Mountfields, though he had been born at Woore near Market Drayton and was a builder by trade. He had served part-time in the Shropshire Artillery Volunteers before joining the KSLI National Reserve. A son of his had also recently died of pneumonia whilst serving on the Western Front.

Captain Willoughby Lynch Cotton (165) also lived at Mountfields and also died of pneumonia, on 6 January 1918, aged 54. He came, however, from a very different strata of society to Private Peel and was perhaps the 'noblest' Great War casualty buried in the Cemetery. He was a member of a Cheshire landowning family headed by Viscount Combermere and the son of Army **Captain Hugh Stapleton Cotton (165)** — beside whom he was buried — who lived at Radnor House in Belle Vue (taken over during the war as an Army Pay Office). Willoughby was commissioned into the Shropshire Militia, later to become the KSLI's 3rd Battalion. Before the war he lived in Weston Rhyn near Oswestry, moving into Shrewsbury when, on 5 August 1914, he was appointed Recruiting Officer for the town. The Army's recruiting efforts had strong backing from the Borough Council — Shrewsbury's mayor at the outbreak of war, Major C.R.B. Wingfield, was a brother officer in the KSLI 3rd Battalion — and the introduction of conscription in 1916 kept the recruiting offices in work. Most men of the town who joined the Army in the war did so during his time in charge. His last illness came after catching a chill in his office just after New Year's Day 1918. He left a widow, and a daughter from his first marriage.

Captain Joshua Bowers Hughes-Games MC (161) of the Durham Light Infantry died from influenza at the Nursing Institution, 1 Quarry Place, on 17 October 1917 aged 30. His home was not far away at 8 Quarry Place, and his father, a clergyman who buried him, lived at Clifton, Bristol. Captain Hughes-Games was a pupil of Shrewsbury School from 1902 to 1907, during which time he helped in rescuing much of the library's contents during the fire of 1905, and left as Head Boy when he gained a Classical Scholarship to Queen's College, Cambridge. Before the war he was Assistant Master at the minor public school in London known as the Forest School. He was commissioned in the Durham Light Infantry in October 1914 and served in Salonika (where he gained his Military Cross), and in France where he was twice wounded and also gassed. He was in hospital for 20 months before being discharged and had just taken a temporary master's post at his old school for the Autumn term when he died.

Another man with a Shrewsbury School background was **Major Malcolm Douglas (210)** of the 46th Battery Machine Gun Corps, who died in Queen Alexandra's Military Hospital, Millbank, London, from pneumonia following influenza, on 17 November 1918, aged 26. He had been taken ill in his hotel whilst on leave in the city. His home was Oakleigh on Belle Vue Road and he was educated privately in Llandudno and, from 1907 to 1909, at Shrewsbury

School. He was employed by the National Provincial Bank in London before the war and, after the outbreak, enlisted in the 16th Middlesex Regiment (known as the Public Schools Battalion) before being commissioned in the 11th (St Helen's) Battalion, South Lancashire Regiment. He transferred to the new Machine Gun Corps in November 1915 and, after qualifying as a machine gunner at a course held at the Vickers works, went to the Western Front in 1916. He spent a year at the front (during which time he was mentioned in despatches by Sir Douglas Haig, Commander-in-Chief of the British forces) before being invalided home with trench fever. On recovery he joined his unit at Grantham and qualified as a machine gunnery instructor only one mark behind the top student. He then returned to the front, was promoted to Major in June 1918 and took part in the attack on the St Quinten canal on 29 September in the final push to remove the Germans from France. Said to have an ambition to lead his men into Germany, his last illness prevented him reporting back to his unit on 11 November, which transpired to be Armistice Day.

The circumstances in which servicemen of the 1914–18 War died varied greatly. **Private William Paskin (10)** committed suicide by cutting his throat in the wash-house at Copthorne Barracks on 21 June 1916 at the age of 26. Paskin was a recent recruit from Hanley, Stoke-on-Trent and was apparently deluded that he was about to be punished — the inquest was told that he said to the soldier who found him: 'They said I had to be shot!' — although he reportedly had no punishment listed on his conduct sheet. **Private Edward Martin (187),** 3rd KSLI, died at Copthorne Barracks in February 1916 aged 32, from injuries received in a barrack room brawl over a game of Crown and Anchor (the only type of gambling allowed in the Army). He was punched by another soldier, fell backwards and hit his head on the foot of a bed. The inquest returned a 'misadventure' verdict. Martin was a native of the Clee Hill area of South Shropshire. **Pioneer George William Rogers (2)** of the Royal Engineers died in hospital at Ramsgate, Kent, in August 1918 aged 35, after being run over by a taxi cab when he and another soldier were walking back to camp after an evening's drinking in the town. Rogers' home was in Castlefields and he had served in the Shropshire Yeomanry in the Boer War and been in the Sappers since 1916.

Corporal Arthur Reginald Harry Davies (150), 6th KSLI, died at the Nursing Institution in Quarry Place on 19 July 1917 at the age of 27 from the effects of wounds received at Auberidge during the battle of Loos in September 1915; in an infantry charge he was shot through an arm before an exploding shell left him with paralysing shrapnel wounds in the shoulder and spine. He lay so long on the ground before his eventual rescue that he later recalled that a number of German soldiers passed over him, thinking he was dead. He was educated at Wrekin College and before enlistment was working for the Shrewsbury Borough Electricity Works. He was also a member of Pengwern Boat Club and Shrewsbury Amateur Football Club. Davies joined the Shrewsbury Pals in September 1914. **Private Thomas Reginald Groves (190)** also died from wounds received at the front. He served in the Coldstream Guards and died at his parents' home at 4 Holywell Terrace, Abbey Foregate on 29 May 1916 aged 32. He was the son of town councillor George Groves and grandson of former Shrewsbury mayor **Thomas Groves (190)** (buried in a neighbouring vault). Private Groves had been employed as a Post Office telephone clerk and was for seven years a part-time Territorial in the Shropshire Yeomanry until a training accident at Oswestry left him unable to follow his civilian job and he was granted a temporary pension. By the time war broke out he had recovered sufficiently to join the more rigorously trained Guards and went with his battalion to the Western Front. He was the only survivor of a group of men who were half buried alive by an exploding 'Jack Johnson' shell (nicknamed such after the ex-world heavyweight boxing champion), only being rescued after two or three days having waived a pole to draw attention. The injuries he sustained, however, led to him being invalided home and ultimately to his death, of which his family gravestone modestly records: 'gave up his life ... after 8 months active service in France'.

The death of **Private Arthur Clement Patrick Eaton (36)** is given added poignancy by the fact that it took place on 11 November 1918, the day of the Allied/German Armistice. Private Eaton had been called up earlier that

The Armoury, c.1916, when used to house Belgian refugees

same year and served in the 3rd/4th Battalion of the KSLI. He died aged 18 in Pembroke Dock Camp Military Hospital in South Wales. Similarly **Private Walter Jarrett (198)**, 3rd KSLI, died at his home in School Terrace, Ditherington on 28 June 1919, the day the Peace Treaty of Versailles was signed, legally ending the war; he was aged 44. **Private Jesse Bedwell (157)** of the Royal Army Service Corps died at the County Asylum at Shelton on 3 July 1921, aged 42. The Asylum — later known as the Salop Mental Hospital — took victims of shellshock (first experienced in great numbers amongst soldiers on the Western Front) as well as brain-damaging head wounds and other more general mental illnesses.

Many Belgian civilian refugees and soldiers came to Britain in the wake of the German invasion of their homeland, which triggered Britain's entry into the war. In Shrewsbury a former armoury near Wenlock Road (which gave its name to the nearby Armoury Gardens) was opened as a hostel for them, which it remained until after the war. In 1922 the building was bought by Morris's, taken down and re-erected near the Welsh Bridge as their new bakery. Today it is a public house known once again as The Armoury. Two Belgian soldiers — one from each of the country's two language groups — were buried in the Cemetery. **Theodore Jacques Delmay (83)**, a Walloon (French speaker) of the 4th Volunteer Regiment, died of tuberculosis at the former Atcham Union Workhouse aged 26 and was buried on 2 December 1915. A native of Liège, the first major city to fall to the Germans, he fought in the rearguard action which led to the evacuation of Antwerp. He was injured by a German rifle butt in the chest during hand-to-hand fighting and suffered exposure which brought on his illness. In 1923 his body was exhumed and reburied in Liège.

Kamiel Versyck (66), a Fleming and Soldat (Private) in the 3rd Regiment of 'Jagers Te Voet' (the equivalent of an English light infantry regiment), hanged himself in his cell at Shrewsbury Prison on 5 May 1916 aged 26. He had been on remand, awaiting trial on a charge of stabbing an English civilian with a knife 'with intent to commit grievous bodily harm' at Croxton, Staffordshire and, at his own request, worked alone in his cell making mailbags. He hanged himself with a cord used in the work. At the Inquest, the jury foreman commented that Versyck may have been under the misapprehension that he would hang for this offence in England. Born at Steankerke, he lived near Brussels until August 1914 when the Germans invaded Belgium and he was sent with his regiment to the frontier. In his suicide note, translated by **Jean Van De Pol (185)**, a Shrewsbury resident of Dutch nationality who worked as a voluntary welfare officer to the local Belgian refugee community, he wrote of his experiences: 'I went to a place near Antwerp. In one of the nights many Belgians and Germans were left. That night the water came high and English men came to help me.' His grave has a standard Belgian military headstone which incorporates the Belgian tricolour and a black cross. The inscription is in Flemish on a cast iron plaque and depicts his medals.

After the United States entered the war on the Allied side in 1917, an expeditionary force of the US Army was sent to the Western Front. Britain's training and hospital facilities were made available to the American troops who gradually arrived in France from June that year but began fighting in earnest in the summer of 1918, when the Germans were beginning to retreat after their failed Spring Offensive. Two US Expeditionary Force soldiers, who

A First World War Prisoner of War camp establsihed in the Midland Yard just south of the abbey, which can be espied through the trees in the background

both died at Berrington War Hospital (the former Atcham Union Workhouse at Cross Houses), were buried together on 2 November 1918 in section 192 of the Cemetery. They were **Private Reginald Banwell** aged 26, and **Private William Henne** aged 24. In 1920, in line with the a long standing policy of burying its military dead in dedicated cemeteries, their bodies were exhumed and repatriated to the United States.

The First World War was the first time since the Napoleonic War that Britain was host to prisoners of war. In 1914 a prisoner of war camp was established in the disused Midland Carriage Works in Coleham, subsequently called Abbey Wood Camp. Because of labour shortage caused by conscription, German prisoners were employed to help on farms, in quarries and, in 1918, to set up an RAF aerodrome at Monkmoor. Seven German prisoners of war were buried in Shrewsbury Cemetery in scattered plots. In 1963 their bodies were exhumed and reburied in the German Military Cemetery at Cannock Chase which is operated by the German War Graves Commission.

Gustav Hermann (83) died aged 36 at the Royal Salop Infirmary from the effects of a shrapnel wound to the head. He was buried on 21 November 1914 and his was the first military funeral of the War to take place in Shrewsbury Cemetery, coming as it did some seven days before the death of the first British soldier to be buried there (from the outset the War Office decided that prisoners of war were to be buried with full military honours). Hermann was a 'Soldat' (or private) and his coffin was carried by four German officers and draped with the German national flag. A detachment of KSLI National Reserve soldiers, who acted as guards at the Abbey Wood Camp, accompanied the coffin and provided a firing party. Hermann being Roman Catholic, Canon Moriarty from the Catholic Cathedral on Town Walls read the burial service.

Anton Engelke (83), an Unterohizier (a Non Commissioned Officer) with the Landwehr Regiment number 18, died at Abbey Wood Camp and was buried on 22 June 1915, aged 32. He belonged to the German equivalent of our Territorial Army and was also a Roman Catholic. Of his funeral procession, with twelve German prisoners of war acting as bearers and an escort of National Reserve men with fixed bayonets, the *Shrewsbury Chronicle* reported:

> The route to the Cemetery was crowded, but there was no hostile demonstration, and as the hearse passed along women could be heard sympathetically remarking 'He was some poor mother's son', 'He's paid the penalty poor chap', and so forth: While men invariably respectfully removed their hats as the coffin passed by. The sight of the German prisoners, however, raised no such feelings of compassion, and in Coleham especially, women were very uncomplimentary in their comments.

With the British press demonising Germans through exaggerated reports of atrocities in Belgium, and the outrage caused by the sinking of the *Lusitania* a month before, it would not be surprising if the comments had included 'Huns' or 'murderers'.

Also buried in the Cemetery were **Frederick Heinrich Eschrich (83)** and **Fritz Schweitzer (129)**, who died in April and August 1918 respectively. **Herbert Otto Wilhelm Lamprecht (97)** and **Richard Wilhelm Reinmath (97)** both died in November 1918, but after hostilities had ended.

12   LEST WE FORGET

In October 1939, shortly after the outbreak of the Second World War, Shrewsbury Cemetery was extended on its west side with the extension divided into twenty consecrated plots. In 1940, a large portion of Plot 10 was set aside for the graves of British Commonwealth servicemen and women who died in this area during the course of the War and up to 1947. Shropshire had several airfields at the time, an infantry regimental depot and a military hospital. The graves in Plot 10 of Shrewsbury Cemetery highlight an aspect of war which is easily overlooked. Those killed on active service abroad were generally buried near to where they fell, those buried in our local cemetery, however, were equally tragic casualties of war, some dying of their war wounds (after being shipped home for hospital treatment), others died in accidents locally or from illness. Sadly, some — unable to go on — committed suicide.

War Graves Commission plot in Shrewsbury Cemetery

Besides 47 Commonwealth servicemen and women, 23 Italians and 27 German servicemen are also buried in the same war graves plot, as well as two Poles. The Italians and Germans had been captured by the Allies and died as Prisoners of War in captivity in and around Shropshire. The nearest PoW camp was at Shelton Road and one man was buried from there, but the largest number (15) were from Iscoyd Park near Whitchurch. Others were held in camps at Donnington, Ludlow, Wem and Condover. In a cemetery which is otherwise owned by the Borough Council, Plot 10 is owned and managed by the Commonwealth War Graves Commission, who provide each grave with a standard Portland Stone headstone.

Each German headstone has an inscribed Mantua Cross (known in England as an Iron Cross) as a symbol of nationality; the headstones acknowledge that they died as servicemen of their country. There are two main phases to the German burials. The first, between July 1944 and January 1945, coincides with the closing stages of the War, when many Germans were captured or surrendered during Allied advances in Italy and north-west Europe. The second

phase, September 1945 to March 1947, was during the immediate post-war period when Prisoners of War were awaiting repatriation, which was only finally agreed in 1948 for those in Anglo-American hands. During this period, at a time of labour shortage, German prisoners were directed to do supervised work on farms and in certain light industries.

Four of the German prisoners died in military hospitals, two on farms, one in a road accident and the remainder in PoW camps. Their ages ranged from 19 to 47 years. Apart from three Roman Catholics, the men were all Protestants. Their burials were conducted with appropriate religious rites by local Anglican or Roman Catholic clergy, though in 1946/47 German service chaplains, who were themselves PoWs, were allowed to officiate. The intriguingly named

One of the Italian War Graves

Abdulajew Faisula, apparently of Arab origin, was himself buried with Protestant rites; he died on 11 January 1945.

The Italian PoWs, like the Germans, were all non-commissioned, ranging from Private ('Soldato') to Sergeant. One was a 'Carabinieri', which suggests he was a member of the armed military and civil police force of Italy. The majority of the Italians would have been captured in the North Africa campaign when Italy was at war on the side of Nazi Germany. The period ended when Mussolini was deposed and the Italian government, rid of his dictatorship, made peace with the Allies. However, because the Germans took over the 'defence' of Italy and occupied it, repatriation of Italian prisoners had to wait at least until the end of hostilities with Germany. The first Italians were buried in Shrewsbury in 1943, the last in 1946.

Of members of the British and Commonwealth forces of that period buried in the Cemetery, the youngest was **Private Willam J. Cotter** of the RASC (the Army's Service Corps) who was killed in a 'flying bomb' raid on London on 28 July 1944, aged 18. His body was brought to Shrewsbury for burial

as his father was a serving non-commissioned officer in the King's Shropshire Light Infantry, living at the time in quarters at Copthorne Barracks. The oldest was **Private Charles Burchett** of the Pioneer Corps, a unit raised in October 1939 primarily from ex-soldiers still able to wield a pick and shovel. He died at Copthorne Military Hospital (part of what is now the Royal Shrewsbury Hospital) on 27 February 1946 aged — according to the Cemetery Register — 68! A man of this age could well have previously served in the Boer War, let alone the 1914–18 War. No details of his military career appear to have survived but he was born in North London and enlisted when living in Surrey.

There are three servicewomen buried in the War Graves section of Shrewsbury Cemetery. Volunteer *The gravestone of Abdulajew Faisula* **Constance Barnicut** was a native

117

of Huddersfield, though her home was in Bushey, Hertfordshire at the time. She was aged 40 when she died in the Salop Mental Hospital at Shelton. **Private Nora Trowell** was born in Bury, Lancashire, she was a member of the ATS (Auxiliary Territorial Service) and died aged 21 in 1944 at Copthorne Hospital. **Sister Marion Isabel Tonge** of the Queen Alexandra's Imperial Military Nursing Service died at Shenley Military Hospital, Hertfordshire in October 1942, aged 32. She was a native of Shropshire, however, and it was from her home county that she had enlisted. The QAIMNS was formed in 1902 and its nurses served principally on hospital ships and in military hospitals.

Undoubtedly the most 'noble' casualty of the Second World War in the Cemetery was **Lieutenant Edward Courteney Ferrers Vyvyan**, whose family were primarily Cornish land-owners, headed by a Baronet. He was born in London in 1887, graduated from Cambridge, was a Barrister of the Inner Temple and served in the 1914–18 War as a Captain in the King's Royal Rifle Corps. He returned to service in the Pioneer Corps and died on duty at Donnington camp on 14 November 1940, aged 53. His family history in *Burke's Peerage* states that he was killed in action, though it must be said there is no record of Donnington ever being subjected to enemy air raids. The highest ranking officer buried in a war grave in Shrewsbury Cemetery is **Major William Frank Heyland**, also of the Pioneers. He was accidentally killed in December 1942 on Wyle Cop, when his bicycle collided with a bus. He was aged 53, had been born in India and served as a regular through the First World War. He retired in 1922 and went on to the 'Reserve'. He farmed in Pirbright, Surrey, before returning to the Army after the outbreak of the Second World War.

Heyland was not the only casualty of a road accident buried in the War Graves plot: **Lance Corporal Dennis George Ellis** died on 20 December 1940 of his injuries, after such an accident, in the Cottage Hospital, Dumbarton in Scotland. His home was in Mountfields, Shrewsbury and his body was brought back to the town for burial. He had joined the Army in 1936 and served in Egypt before the War. A champion swimmer in both civilian and Army life, Ellis specialised in the breast stroke and in Shrewsbury had held the Bibby Swimming Cup for four years in succession. He surrendered the Cup when he enlisted, but continued to win cups and medals and represented the British Army against Egypt. **Lance Sergeant Sidney Mansell Adams** of the Royal Artillery, died on 26 April 1941 in the Royal Salop Infirmary of injuries received in an accident between Shrewsbury and Church Stretton, when his motor cycle collided with an Army lorry in convoy. Born in Dudley, his family moved to Shrewsbury when he was a child. He served as a Motor Transport Driver in France during the First World War and in 1919, when living in Coleham, was in the Royal Berkshire Regiment. He worked on the railways in civilian life and was recalled in 1939. Adams was a member of the British Expeditionary Force until evacuated from Dunkirk in 1940, and was employed as a Despatch Rider at the time of his death.

Sergeant William Jones died a couple of years after Adams, in January 1943, but in remarkably similar circumstances — his motorcycle also collided with an Army lorry in convoy near Church Stretton. Sergeant Jones was born and brought up near Llanymynech on the Welsh border, was a Regular with the King's Shropshire Light Infantry from 1933 to 1938 and had served in India. He moved to Shrewsbury in 1939 and on the outbreak of war was recalled to his regiment and was employed as an Instructor to the Shropshire Home Guard. The jury at the Inquest into his death heard that he had been riding his motorcycle at the back of the convoy on Church Stretton by-pass, the machine was seen to wobble and he was thrown off and rolled down the road as the motorcycle skidded away. The Lance Corporal in charge of the convoy found Jones with severe head injuries and flagged down a passing motorist to call an ambulance. Jones was taken to Copthorne Military Hospital but died there later. Evidence was given to the Inquest that he was an experienced rider but that the road only had a temporary surface and was full of pot-holes; a verdict of accidental death was recorded.

Pilot Officer Douglas Ford of the RAF was a passenger in a US Army jeep when he died on 20 August 1943. He and another RAF officer, who also lost his life, were taking a lift from Shrewsbury back to their base at RAF Shawbury when the jeep crashed into a telegraph pole on Ellesmere Road, Shrewsbury. Ford, who came from Leicester, died two days later in the Royal Salop Infirmary. Finally, **Gunner Frederick Raymond Robertson** (of the 59th Newfoundland Heavy Regiment, Royal Artillery) died in 1944 three days after a road accident near Newtown in Montgomeryshire. He fell against an oncoming lorry during a road-side brawl with Italian Prisoners of War. An open verdict was recorded at his Inquest because of uncertainty about whether he fell accidentally or was deliberately pushed by the Italians, who fled the scene. To further complicate matters, it was clear that Robertson had been drinking whilst off duty. Witnesses reported that the fight was provoked when he saw the Italian prisoners, who were 'on liberty', talking to a local girl. Robertson came from Humbermouth in Newfoundland. Although now a Canadian province, Newfoundland was then a Commonwealth dominion in its own right, its soldiers therefore came under British rather than Canadian command.

Two of the German PoWs buried in Shrewsbury Cemetery also died as a result of motor accidents, and within weeks of each other. **Erwin Korff** was aged 23 when he was accidentally killed on 3 January 1947 at Shelton Road camp. He was helping guide an RAF lorry into a garage for repairs when he was crushed between the vehicle and a swing door. **Johann Rottenkolber** (known as Hans) died almost instantly at the scene of an accident on the main Madeley to Bridgnorth road near the village of Sutton Maddock on 13 December 1946. He was a passenger in a lorry taking a group of Germans to work on farms when it collided side-on with an RAF lorry on the icy road.

There were a number of RAF bases in Shropshire during the Second World War and at least eight of the servicemen buried in Shrewsbury Cemetery died in flying accidents. **RAF Warrant Officer Edward Creber** was born in Scotland but moved with his family to Shrewsbury where they lived in Mousecroft Lane. He was educated at the Priory Boys'

The gravestone of Johann Rottenkolber

School and then Harold's College, London. Creber joined the RAF on the outbreak of war in 1939, and was variously stationed in Northern Ireland and South Africa as a navigation instructor, before returning to Britain. Flying was evidently something of a family interest as his elder brother was training with the RAF in Canada and his younger brother was an RAF cadet. On 15 February 1944, he was leading a training flight in his Whitley Mk V bomber,

Stiperstones village with Mytton Dingle behind, site of Edward Creber's fatal crash

which was towing a glider. They flew over the Stiperstones hills towards the south when they were disturbed by a current of wind. The glider cast-off and landed safely in nearby Hope Valley, but the bomber's wing tip caught the steep hillside and it crashed into Mytton Dingle, disintegrating on impact and leaving wreckage over a wide area. Local people rushed to the site, but to no avail, and all five members of the crew had died before help arrived. Wallace Evans from Stiperstones village later recalled the event in *Never on a Sunday* published by the Shropshire Mines Trust in 2000:

> We ran all the way up Mytton Dingle. When we got there it was an inferno. I shall never forget this lad lying there, he'd been thrown clear but his back was broken and his neck. There was just a flicker of life there. Every lace in his boot was split as was his belt ... The scar was on the hill for years and years. I went up some time later and found a half crown and an old penny and a ha'penny. I've got them in an old tin and I'd never spend them.

Sergeant/Pilot Cyril George Pritchard was killed near Godstone in Surrey on his way to or from a bombing mission to Germany (the details remain obscure). He was a single man who lived with his parents in Sentinel Gardens, Harlescott, and joined the RAF in 1937. He was initially employed as a wireless operator before training as a pilot and had taken part in several operational flights before his final one in April 1942; he was 23 years old. **Sergeant/Observer Edwin W.E. Jones** died in August of the same year at the RAF Hospital in Ely, also as the result of a flying accident of which the details are unknown. He was a native of Shrewsbury and lived in Berwick Avenue. In his childhood he had been a boy scout and was later employed at the Sugar Beet factory at Allscott near Wellington. Being part of the agricultural industry, this work excused him from conscription. Nevertheless he initially served in the Home Guard and then volunteered for RAF flying duties in June 1941.

Aircraftsman (Class 1) **John R.L. Edwards** was an excellent swimmer and in 1937 was presented with the Royal Humane Society's 'Certificate on vellum' for saving the life of a young girl — Sylvia Parry — from the River Severn, near the weir. He was also a regular attender at All Saints' church in Castlefields, where he lived with his parents, and was a member of the choir for many years. He joined the RAF on the day war was declared and was described as 'an enthusiastic member with excellent prospects of promotion.' Sadly, these ambitions were not to be realised, as he was killed in a flying accident at the RAF station, Sutton Bridge in Norfolk on 13 October 1940. **Allan Francis** moved to Sundorne Crescent in Shrewsbury with his parents in 1939 just before the outbreak of hostilities. In 1942 Allan joined the ATC (Air Training Corps) and volunteered for the RAF as soon as he reached the age of

18. He 'passed out' as a Sergeant/Air Gunner in 1943 but was to die when his plane crashed on farmland at Talke, near Kidsgrove, Staffordshire.

At ten past midnight on 3 March 1943 an horrific accident occurred in the grounds of Acton Reynolds girls' school, near Grinshill, when a Lancaster bomber crashed killing all seven members of its crew. They were training for night-time bombing missions and none had any operational experience except their captain and pilot **Sergeant Edgar C. Fulton**. Fulton, as well as two of his colleagues — **Sergeant Ross C. Graham** of New South Wales and **Sergeant Edward J. Murphy** who hailed from Victoria — were all serving with the Royal Australian Air Force. Also buried in Shrewsbury Cemetery as a result of the accident was **Sergeant Thomas P.G. Milledy**, the crew's flight engineer. Sergeant Milledy came from Cambridge and was based at a training airfield in Leicestershire. All four were in their twenties. The bodies of the other three crew members (Sergeants Peter Bacon, Roderick Kerr and Ronald Oldfield, all serving with the RAF) are likely to have been returned to their home area for burial.

Volunteers from Commonwealth countries across the world came forward in their thousands to support the Allied cause in the Second World War. **Private Nganda Kadugala** was a member of the African Pioneer Corps and must therefore have been a native of Uganda, Kenya or Tanganyika (now Tanzania). He died in Copthorne Military Hospital at the age of 30 in 1945. African soldiers such as Private Kadugala served not only in African campaigns but also the Middle and Far East.

Two Poles who died in Shropshire as members of their own armed forces under British military control, are also buried in the Cemetery. **Flying Officer Felino Paul Nowak** of the Polish Air Force died on Haughmond Hill near Shrewsbury on 9 November 1941 at the age of 28. After service with the Polish Army from 1937 to 1938, he worked in the cotton trade until Germany invaded Poland, when he saw much fighting with the 59th Infantry Regiment. Escaping from Poland via Hungary and Yugoslavia to France, he once again joined the Polish forces, under French control. At some time during this period it appears that he became a prisoner of war, but little is then known of his life until he made his way to England via Spain and Portugal and joined the Polish air crew training centre at Hucknall, Derbyshire in July 1942. On 1 September 1943 he was commissioned as a Pilot Officer and was posted to 60 Operational Training Unit at High Ercall in October of the following year.

He was to meet his death a matter of weeks later on the night of 9 November. At around 1am, just after his sixth take-off, the Mosquito he was flying veered into a sharp turn and went into a spiral dive before crashing and exploding on impact at Haughmond Farm near Shrewsbury. Wreckage was spread over a wide area, with burning debris landing on the front yard of the farm and a main wheel coming to rest in a nearby garden. The circumstances of the crash point to engine failure at low speed, something which is almost impossible for any pilot to handle even an experienced one such as Nowak who had over 500 flying hours behind him. Flying Officer Nowak was a Roman Catholic, which explains his burial in Shrewsbury Cemetery rather than High Ercall churchyard. Some years ago Delphing Nowak, Felino's widow, visited Haughmond Farm with her daughter.

His countryman, **Private Eugeniusz Wojdasiewicz**, was to die three years later after the end of the War. A member of the Polish Army, he was stationed at Donnington camp and on 17 January 1947 shot himself in a field near the camp. What was behind his tragic suicide remains a mystery. No Inquest report has come to light.

Sadly, his was not the only suicide amongst members of the armed forces based in Shropshire. **Private John Robertson** of the Royal Army Ordnance Corps (RAOC) also shot himself with his own rifle, at Shrewsbury Railway Station. He was a single man who lived with his sister in the East Ancoats district of Manchester. He had worked as a Railway Porter until he enlisted in June 1941 and killed himself on 31 July of the same year. Robertson was based at Donnington and had over-stayed a period of leave by some seven days. It was thought at the time that his suicide was caused by unhappiness at life away from home.

Undoubtedly the most bizarre story here is that of **Private John Cain** of the London Scottish. Even records made at the time are confused: the Cemetery Register has his rank as Lance Corporal rather than Private, and the *Shrewsbury Chronicle* report of his death records his name as John Vincent (he was known to have used several aliases). Private Cain shot himself with his own pistol on 7 August 1940 in the grounds of Ranslett House, Eaton Constantine near Shrewsbury. He was being apprehended at the time by police

Ranslett House

123

after going absent without leave from his Territorial Unit in London. He was 33 years old and came from a middle class family, but was blighted with mental instability and pathological dishonesty. He had been expelled from several boarding schools and served prison sentences for burglary and cheque fraud. Between 1927 and 1931 he lived in New Zealand where his family attempted to help him settle, but he returned to England after being gaoled there. His family then set him up as a travelling salesman in a business which he left in 1936 after losing trade through dishonesty and financial mismanagement. In 1937 he was declared bankrupt with debts of £10,000 and later absconded to Malaya before being arrested and gaoled again.

He joined the Territorial Army sometime after his release and before the outbreak of war in 1939. His military duties seem to have been largely unaffected by his instability and complex private life until he abruptly left London with a woman friend, alleging England had been invaded! Five days later he shot himself near the small Shropshire village of Eaton Constantine. The Inquest was delayed to allow Special Branch police investigations, because he variously purported to be an RAF officer, Royal Navy Commander, linked to British Intelligence and, finally, a German spy. His address was given as 48 Berkeley Street, London and he left an estranged widow and children.

Two of the Italian PoWs buried in the Cemetery were briefly in the local headlines, though for very different reasons. **Caporal Maggiore Silvio Garofalo** drowned while bathing in the River Severn at Shelton Roughs on 29 May 1944. He was known to be a strong swimmer and it was believed he fainted in the water when attempting to get back to the shore. The Cemetery Register gives his abode as Sherrifhales PoW camp (near Newport, Shropshire), but his death occurred while he was 'on liberty' from the camp on Shelton Road, Shrewsbury. Three days later, **Soldato Leopoldo Santarpia** died — he was fatally stabbed with a work knife in a brawl with a fellow PoW in the cobbler's workshop at Sherrifhales camp. His assailant was later convicted of manslaughter.

Hostilities in the Second World War finally ceased on 15 August 1945 with the Japanese surrender. The last serviceman to be buried in the Cemetery before then was **Sapper Frederick Wilkins** of the Royal Engineers, a Nottingham man who died on 28 July 1945 in Copthorne Military Hospital; he was 35 years old. The last PoW to be buried while Allied/German hostilities took place still in his native country was **Gaetano Gagliardi**, a Private in the Italian army. The year of birth on his headstone suggests that he was aged 28 or 29, however the Cemetery Register records his age as 24, suggesting that he may have volunteered giving a false age. He died in Copthorne Hospital on 23 March 1945 and German troops in Italy surrendered just a few weeks later on 2 May.

Looking back at the lives of those who lie buried in Shrewsbury Cemetery has been an absorbing exercise. I have found many of their stories to be fascinating, informative and even inspiring. The Cemetery, however, has not completed the service it has provided for the people of Shrewsbury since 1856. Burials still take place there on a regular basis and will do into the foreseeable future. Stories will still be told and lives remembered with the inevitable mix of sadness and joy, as they always have been and always will.

Further Reading and Selected Bibliography

Much of the background information for this book came from the substantial and well-organised resources of Shropshire Archives in Castle Gates, Shrewsbury. Of particular value were back copies of the *Shrewsbury Chronicle* and other local newspapers, the *Shropshire Magazine* and the *Shropshire Notes and Queries* series. Numerous books were consulted, of which I hope the following will prove to be a useful representative sample:

Best, Geoffery *Mid-Victorian Britain 1851–75*, Fontana Paperbacks, 1979.

Brooks, Chris *Mortal Remains – The History and Present State of the Victorian and Edwardian Cemetery*, Wheaton Publishers Ltd, 1989.

Charlesworth, Michael *JB Oldham of Oldham's Hall 1882–1962*, Greenbank Press, 1996.

Charlesworth, Michael (ed.) *Heads and Tales: Salopiana 1900–1950*, Greenbank Press, 2000.

Coles, Gladys Mary *The Flower of Light: A Biography of Mary Webb*, Gerald Duckworth and Co, 1978.

Curl, James Stevens *The Victorian Celebration of Death*, Sutton Publishing, 2000.

Dickson *et al Shrewsbury School Football and the Old Salopian FC*, 1995.

Elderwick, David *50 Shropshire Celebrities Past and Present,* Imprint 1989.

Elliott, Douglas J. *Policing Shropshire 1836–1967*, Brewin Books, 1984.

Fletcher, Revd J.M.J. *Mrs Wightman of Shrewsbury – the story of a pioneer in temperance work*, Longmans Green and Co, 1906.

Jones, Mike *Breathe on 'em Salop,* Yore Publications, 1995.

Newton, John A. *Search for a Saint: Edward King*, Epworth Press, 1977.

Palmer, Alan *The Banner of Battle – The Story of the Crimean War,* Weidenfeld and Nicolson, 1987.

Sinker, Charles (ed.) *Hilda Murrell's Nature Diaries*, Collins, 1987.

Warsop, Keith *The Early FA Cup Finals and the Southern Amateurs*, Tony Brown, 2004.

Index

Also from Logaston Press

The Churches of Shropshire & their Treasures
by John Leonard

This book explores 320 parish churches of Shropshire, half of them medieval. Chapters guide the reader through changing architectural styles, from Anglo-Saxon origins to the 21st century and then detail the treasures of the churches, including towers and spires, porches roofs, sculpture, fonts, memorials and monuments, stained glass, rood-screens, pulpits, pews and chancel furnishings. The county is then divided into geographical areas, with descriptions of all the individual churches in each area.

John Leonard is a retired consultant physician who lives in Shropshire and has written numerous books on churches.

ISBN 1 904396 19 4 (978 1 904396 19 2)
336 pages, over 530 illustrations   Price £12.95

Vernacular Buildings of Shropshire
by Madge Moran

Over a period spanning thirty years, Madge Moran has visited, decyphered and recorded many of Shropshire's vernacular buildings that owe their origins to the period commencing c.1200. This book brings together that work, with the exception of the area around Whitchurch which has been covered in the earlier publication Vernacular Buildings of Whitchurch and Area and their occupants.

Initial chapters track the changes from buildings designed with defence in mind to first-floor halls of both stone and timber-framing and thence to ground-floor halls. Cruck buildings are given their own chapter, as are box-framed and jettied houses. Roof construction, with its various forms across Shropshire, is also accorded its own section. The changes from the fully developed three-part plan medieval house with its clearly defined solar and service ends or wings, screens passage and open hall to what may be called the 'early modern' house, fully floored, with a central entrance and displaying symmetry to a greater or lesser degree, are covered in a chapter on the Transitional House. Other chapters cover wallpaintings and dendrochronology—the latter an important aspect of Madge Moran's work and which provides much of the dating information in this book.

With a concentration of buildings in Ludlow, Shrewsbury and Much Wenlock that have both survived and provided an opportunity for inspection, these towns are given a series of their own chapters which develop themes specific to each town. The wealth of information relating to other properties spread across Shropshire is recorded in a gazetteer which is organised on a parish basis.

ISBN: 1 873827 93 8 (978 1 873827 93 2)
Just under 600 pages, over 1,500 drawings and photographs   Paperback £25

Also from Logaston Press

The Folklore of Shropshire
by Roy Palmer

Shropshire's folklore is presented in a series of themed chapters that encompass landscape, buildings, beliefs, work, seasons, people, music and drama. In the eleven chapters the county's rich store of folklore unfolds in a way that allows you to dip into what most intrigues, or to read from start to finish. Here are stories of mark stones, stone circles, giants, tunnels, dragons, rivers, meres, pools, hills, church sites changed by the devil, vengeful spirits, bull and bear baiting, cockfighting, fairs, herbal remedies and those which involve peculiar activities, minstrels, histriones, waits, charmers and 'cunning folk', ghosts, witches, bountiful cows, of characters such as the early saints, Caratacus, Edric the Wild, Humphrey Kynaston, Jack Mytton and even recent folklore surrounding Hilda Murrell, of tales of the Civil War and of Hopton Quarter, of celebrations and customs surrounding times such as Easter, Christmas, All Souls' Eve, Ascension Day and Palm Sunday along with the likes of 'burning the mawkin', 'tin panning' and wife selling, of rhymes that link villages, ballads that tell of events in the county's past, of folk plays and mummers—to mention just some of what is included.

ISBN 1 904396 16 X (978 1 904396 16 1)
Paperback, 320 pages, over 250 illustrations   Price £12.95

English Architecture to 1900: The Shropshire Experience
by Eric Mercer

This book is a comprehensive guide to Shropshire's architecture, covering church and secular buildings from Anglo-Saxon times to 1900. The range includes Anglican, Catholic and Non-Conformist churches, manor houses and country mansions, the houses of the gentry and yeomanry, town houses, semis and working-class terraces as well as public and communal buildings like railway stations, banks, factories and shops.

Throughout, the intention is to relate regional developments in architecture to a national pattern, to show whether and where Shropshire architecture was in advance of or behind national trends and what distinctive local themes and styles developed. Eric Mercer traces patrons and owners to show how the sources of their wealth, their social aspirations and their political ambitions were the main determinants of the forms of their houses and the nature of their decoration. Ecclesiastical architecture and the styles of public and communal buildings are likewise explained in terms of their social functions and political objectives. In relating the Shropshire experience to national development, he produces a book which not only chronicles the progress of English architecture, but the march of English history

ISBN 1 904396 08 9 (978 1 904396 08 6)
Paperback, 400 pages, 300 illustrations   Price £20

Also from Logaston Press

Some Shropshire Gardens Revisited
by Barbara & Alan Palmer

Written and researched by two dedicated plant and garden lovers, the book describes 50 gardens scattered across Shropshire, most of which are open to the public at various times during the year. The book is crammed with information, observation and pictures that includes: the history and development of each garden; what there is to see; unusual plants and trees; practical advice on the care of plants; ideas for garden design and planting tips. Alan and Barbara Palmer have lived in Shropshire most of their lives making and nurturing three gardens, all of which are open under the National Gardens Scheme.

ISBN: 1 904396 34 8 (978 1 904396 34 5)
Paperback, 128 pages 130 colour photographs   Price £9.95

Cinderallas & Packhorses:
A History of the Shropshire Magistracy
Edited by David J. Cox *and* Barry S. Godfrey

This book provides a very readable and clear picture as to how the early forerunners of Justices of the Peace came about during the reigns of Richard I, Edward I and Edward II, and developed over time. The duties that Justices of the Peace have had to perform have been varied and encompass collecting rates for the repair of bridges, trying those accused of felony and trespass, the regulation of wages and prices, the maintenance of gaols and Houses of Correction, the suppression of disorderly houses, appointment of parish constables, tracing and prosecuting recusants, controlling of riots, fining women deemed to be living idly, judging those killing game, licensing of alehouses, dealing with vagrancy, administration of Poor relief, ensuring the maintenance of a bastard child by its alleged father, ordering people to the stocks or whipping post, dealing with those who uttered a profane oath, judging those who worked on a Sunday, administration of the county rate, the regulation of Turnpike Trusts, supervising the administration of asylums, the formation of police forces and, most recently, dealing with many motoring offences — and that is not a definitive list. These and other duties are all covered. The book successfully explains what was happening nationally, as well as the concerns, issues, and some of the cases that were being dealt with locally. It ends by raising the issues that face the Magistracy today, not least in terms of the professionalisation of the service, and the tension between use of local knowledge and a desire by central government for blanket uniformity.

ISBN: 1 904396 45 3 (978 1 904396 45 1)
Paperback, 112 pages, 30 illustrations   Price £9.95